# War in East Texas

## Regulators vs. Moderators

*For Martha Hook —*

Bill O'Neal

*Bill O'Neal*

University of North Texas Press
Denton, Texas

**For Jessie Lucille Martinez and Bailey Nicole Henderson**
Granddaughters of the author and
descendants of Shelby County pioneers

10 9 8 7 6 5 4 3 2 1

Permissions:
University of North Texas Press
1155 Union Circle #311336
Denton, TX 76203-5017

The paper used in this book meets the minimum
requirements of the American National Standard
for Permanence of Paper for Printed Library
Materials, z39.48.1984. Binding materials have been
chosen for durability.

Library of Congress Cataloging-in-Publication Data is available
from the Library of Congress

ISBN: 978-1-57441-728-9

The electronic edition of this book was made possible by
the support of the Vick Family Foundation.

Originally published in 2006 by the Best of East Texas
Publishers, Lufkin, Texas

# Contents

# Acknowledgments

This book was made possible through the support and encouragement of Bob and Doris Bowman of Lufkin. Bob is a past president of the East Texas Historical Association and Doris is a member of the Association's Board of Directors. The Bowmans long have bolstered the ETHA through their talents, efforts, and resources, and in the fall of 2005 they launched the annual sponsorship of the publication of a book under the imprint of the East Texas Historical Association. Their sole requirement was that each book should focus on East Texas history. The Bowmans enthusiastically approved the concept of this project, and Bob provided me with materials from his extensive files. I am enormously proud that this is the first book in the ETHA series, and I am deeply grateful to Bob and Doris for providing this opportunity.

I am similarly appreciative of the role of Dr. Archie P. McDonald, professor of history at Stephen F. Austin State University and a prolific author. As executive director of the ETHA and editor of the *East Texas Historical Journal,* Dr. McDonald assisted the Bowmans in establishing the series, approved the Regulator-Moderator topic, and improved the manuscript through his editorial expertise. I am happy for the chance to express in print my heartfelt thanks to Archie for his contributions to this book, as well as for his friendship.

At the beginning of this project, I enlisted the aid of Sherri Baker, librarian at Panola College in Carthage. An interlibrary loan specialist of great resourcefulness, Sherri has assisted me with other research projects in the past. As usual she turned up one treasure after another, and I am indebted for her efforts on my behalf. Also in Carthage I was assisted by a longtime friend and enthusiastic local historian, Gerry Graves of the Panola County History and Genealogical Society.

The first seat of Panola County was Pulaski, a log cabin village on the Sabine River. I first visited the townsite, located on private property, a quarter century ago, but when trying to return recently I discovered that logging activities had altered the route. While floundering around in the wilderness, I had an unlikely – and fortunate – meeting with a former student, Gary Payne, who patiently took the trouble to guide me to the secluded location of old Pulaski. When I knocked on a door in southern Panola County to seek directions to Watt Moorman's burial site, I was greeted by another former student, Nannette Eddins, who graciously pointed the way and permitted me to traverse her property.

Another chance encounter occurred when I stopped to photograph the Garrett log cabin, circa 1826, located west of San Augustine. The property was being mowed by Gilbert Garrett of Nacogdoches. It was Gilbert's first visit to the cabin built by his great-grandfather in six weeks, but he cordially gave a tour to a stranger and regaled me with information about his ancestors and their property.

Archaeologist Claude McCrocklin of Shreveport provided me with a detailed copy of his findings at Potter's Point and discussed his conclusions about Robert Potter's home and murder site. At the Jefferson Historical Museum, Gloria Roe produced one source after another from the archives. Gloria photocopied scores of pages and put me in contact with Sammi McSpain, the enthusiastic chairman of the Marion County Historical Commission. Charles Steger of Atlanta, upon hearing of this project, volunteered his help, and provided me with a complete copy of the Ames manuscript.

I was greeted at the Harrison County Historical Museum in Marshall by Joyce Williamson, a stalwart supporter of the ETHA. Archivists Ruth Briggs and George Choate gathered an impressive number of materials for me from the rich collections of the Harrison County Historical Society. The Society president, Judge Ben Z. Grant, suggested leads and related stories from his deep fund of knowledge of his home. On two visits to the Harrison County District Court's office, I was provided with early legal records by another former student, Jason Palmer.

At the Shelby County Historical Museum in Center, Dowell Youngblood related the adventures of his ancestors during the Regulator-Moderator War. Among the materials Dowell copied for me was the unpublished manuscript of Eph Daggett. Ray Jackson skillfully produced copies of photographs from the collection of the

Shelby County Historical Society.

A lifelong citizen of Shelbyville, Johnny Hargrove, has spent decades investigating the Regulator-Moderator War. Johnny has accumulated a vast amount of material on the subject and he has reflected deeply on the causes and chronological order of various events. He enthusiastically shared his information and his conclusions with me, and his generosity greatly enriched this book. I am also grateful to another former student, Shana Brittain of Shelbyville, who informed me about Johnny and arranged our initial meeting.

Willie Earl Tindall, past president of the ETHA, generously loaned me a first edition of John Middleton's *History of the Regulators and Moderators* (1883), and she shared her incomparable fund of knowledge about people and places of San Augustine. John and Betty Oglesbee kindly permitted me to use photographs from their excellent book, *San Augustine: A Texas Treasure*. At the East Texas Research Center at Stephen F. Austin State University, Anne Kendall expertly located numerous useful sources for me. At Fort Jesup, Louisiana, museum curator Linda Freeman enthusiastically explained connections between outlaw gangs in the vicinity of the fort and origins of the Regulator-Moderator War to me.

During the 1980s, while I was researching the Horrell-Higgins feud, I was privileged to have discussions with Dr. C. L. Sonnichsen, author of *I'll Die Before I'll Run* and *Ten Texas Feuds,* among many other works. Doc Sonnichsen was the pre-eminent authority on Texas feuds, and he shared many insights and research experiences with me. I am grateful for his inspiration and encouragement on this fascinating subject.

My wife, Karon, offered many useful suggestions about the manuscript, accompanied me on research trips, and took photos which are used in this book. As always, she efficiently converted my handwritten pages to disk and hardcopy. A time factor was involved in this project, and I could not have met the necessary deadline without Karon's competent and cheerful assistance. For me, Karon defines the term "helpmate," and I am profoundly grateful to her.

_____ Bill O'Neal

# Regulator Faction

## HARRISON COUNTY

Col. William P. Rose
John W. Scott, *his son-in-law*
Col. William T. Boulware

George W. Rembert
Isaac Hughes
Capt. George Davidson

## SHELBY COUNTY

Capt. Charles W. Jackson
Col. Watt Moorman
Helen Daggett Moorman, *his wife*
Eph Daggett
Charles Daggett
Deputy Sheriff John Middleton
Henry Runnels
Stephen Runnels, *his son*
_____ Stanfield, *his hired hand*
Howell Hudson
Col. Leonard Straw
Capt. Joe Smith
Capt. M.T. Johnson
Jerroboam Beauchamp
Capt. John Inman
Elizabeth White, *scout*

_____ Lour, clerk
Sheriff Alfred George
John Myrick
Frank Hooper
Jim Vaughan
Charles L. Mann
Elijah Roberts
Samuel N. Hall
Matthew Brinson
Albert Harris
John Farrar
Franklin Farrar
Mrs. M.T. Johnson, *scout*
Mrs. Nathan Matthews,
  *scout*
Capt. George Standford

# Moderator Faction

## HARRISON COUNTY

Senator Robert M. Potter

Harriet Ames, *his companion*

George Moore, *her brother*

Sheriff John B. Campbell
Judge John Hansford

Peter Whetstone, *founder of Marshall*

Anderson Whetstone, *his son*

Warrick Whetstone, *a younger son*

Daniel Minor
D. Morriss

## SHELBY COUNTY

Joseph W. Goodbread, *land pirate*
Buckskin Bill McFadden
John McFadden

Baily McFadden, *fourteen*
Capt. Edward Merchant
Dr. Levi Ashcroft
John N. Bradley
William Wells Williams, *hired killer*
James Seekers, *hired killer*
Ben Hines, *hired killer*
Sheriff Amon Lewellyn
Col. Jeff Cravens
Jimmy Truitt
Alfred Truitt, *his son*
Everett J. Ritter
Jonathan Anderson
Samuel Todd

Tiger Jim Strickland
Henry Strickland
Squire Humphries, *horse thief*
_____Bledsoe
_____Boatright
_____Burrows, *teacher*
Farrar Metcalf
Amos Hall
Joseph Hall
Jim Hall
Isaac Hall
Mark Haley
Richard Haley
Thomas Haley
Charles Lindsey
Bill Hansbury
Vardeman Duncan

# Regulator-Moderator Country

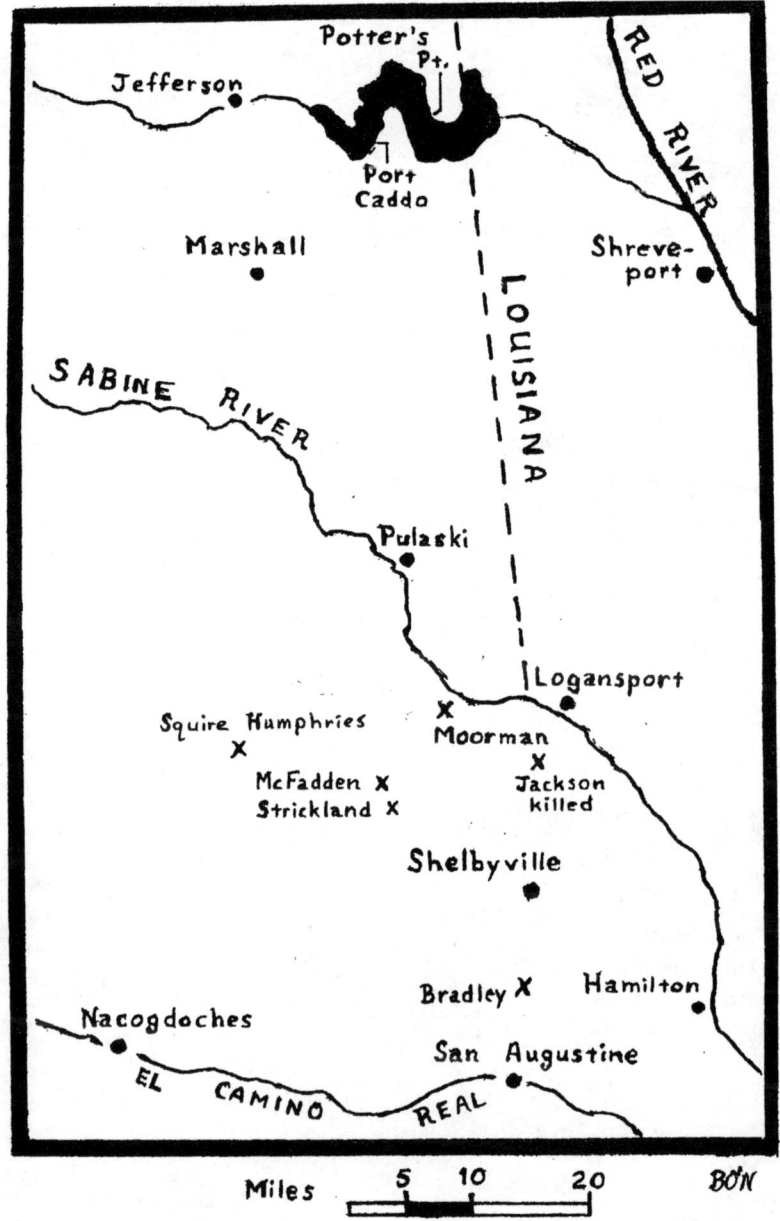

# 1 Murder in Shelbyville

*"When I see him I may scare him
but it will be a damn quick scare."*
—Charles Jackson

One of the foremost land pirates of Shelby County during the late 1830s was Joseph G. Goodbread. Land pirates – men who dealt in fraudulent land titles – congregated in the wilderness county, along with a host of other disreputable characters: fugitives from the nearby United States; horse thieves; slave stealers; counterfeiters; murderers; and assorted other scoundrels.

Goodbread somehow – perhaps through payoffs – gained the cooperation of the Shelby County Board of Commissioners, who provided him "any amount of certificates he required," according to Dr. Levi Ashcroft. A native of North Carolina, Dr. Ashcroft moved to Shelbyville in 1838, the same year as Goodbread. The physician related that in 1839 Goodbread purchased a slave from Alfred George, who often provided the swindler with fictitious names from fraudulent land titles. Goodbread paid George ten headright certificates, a total of 46,050 acres, certainly a lavish price for a single slave, even though both men were aware that the certificates were fraudulent. Dr. Ashcroft added that Goodbread had a wife and several children, and that "with all his faults he was a kind parent and an affectionate husband."[1]

But Goodbread ran afoul of another Shelby County rogue,

Charles W. Jackson, a former steamboat captain. Jackson, a native of Kentucky, operated a small steamboat on the Mississippi and the Red rivers. At Alexandria, on the Red, Captain Jackson killed a local merchant and wounded another in a fight. Jackson quickly steamed away, but a large reward was posted, and authorities tried to arrest him in New Orleans. But Jackson escaped again in his boat and steamed upriver to Shreveport, where he sold the vessel and bought a store. While conducting business at a local river landing, however, Jackson was seized by five men who hustled him onto a steamboat, then headed to Alexandria to collect the reward. But they did not secure Jackson, and when the riverboat drew near a plantation owned by one of his friends, he leaped overboard, swam ashore, and made good another escape.[2]

Jackson headed overland to the Republic of Texas and it was rumored that he hanged someone en route. The fugitive found kindred spirits in Shelby County, so he sent for his family and store goods. Dr. Ashcroft said Jackson had "a reckless bearing and a certain degree of rough eloquence...." Eph Daggett, who lived eighteen miles from Shelbyville, became Jackson's comrade. "Jackson made friends and enemies wherever he went," observed Daggett. "He was always sober, and had a mouthful of teeth, wore a smiling countenance, and always laughed when he wanted or had an intention to fight."[3]

Although a newcomer, Jackson entered the annual race for a seat in the congress of Texas. He lost, but learning the extent of land swindles in the area, "he immediately wrote New Orleans, Houston, Austin and other towns exposing the fraud." Such action inevitably made enemies of Shelby County's land pirates. While returning from Shelbyville to his home one night, Jackson emerged from the woods. A shot was fired from concealment, grazing the back of Jackson's hand. Hearing the gunshot, Mrs. Jackson ran from the cabin and called out to her husband.[4]

"No harm done," he reassured her. A few days later, in April 1841, Jackson received a letter from Joseph Goodbread, warning

"that he had better attend to his business or he would kill him."
Eph Daggett stopped by the cabin on his way home through
Shelbyville after visiting a nearby mill. Jackson showed Daggett the
scar on his hand, read the letter aloud, and asked for advice. While
Daggett was noncommittal, Mrs. Jackson reminded her husband
"that he had had to kill rascals all his life and she expected he would
have to kill a few more before they would let him alone."[5]

Encouraged by his wife's blessing, Jackson waved the letter
and proclaimed that he would kill Goodbread "on first sight."
Daggett told of having his own difficulties with Goodbread until he
"slapped his cheeks" with Goodbread's own knife, thereby "scaring"
the land pirate into terms. "When I see him I may scare him, but it
will be a damn quick scare," Jackson muttered ominously. "He shan't
live. He shan't."[6]

Daggett rode on into Shelbyville, the county seat village
which boasted a log courthouse, a little hotel, and "grog shops."
Daggett soon sighted Goodbread sitting "on an old fashioned horse
rack" and talking with a friend. Dr. Ashcroft contended that Alfred
George, recently elected county sheriff, sent a messenger to tell
Jackson that Goodbread was in town without weapons. An enmity
had developed between Goodbread and Sheriff George over the slave
sold for fraudulent land titles. When the titles were discredited,
Sheriff George stole his old slave back from Goodbread and hid
him in the woods. According to Dr. Ashcroft, Sheriff George relayed
Goodbread's threats to Jackson, and "promised to lend him any
assistance within his power."[7]

Within "a very short time" of Goodbread's arrival, Jackson
rode into town on a fine Kentucky mare, with a rifle at the ready.
"Goodbread, here is your letter. Git up," ordered Jackson from the
saddle. "I am going to answer that letter."

"Jackson, I am unarmed."

"So much the better," replied Jackson coldly, "git up on your
feet."

"Charley, I was mad when I wrote that letter," explained

Goodbread, trying to talk his way out of danger. "I was hasty."

"Stand up," growled Jackson.

Goodbread asked Jackson to allow him to arm himself, and he tried to rise. Jackson "raised his rifle, took deliberate aim, and fired" into Goodbread's chest. The stricken man glared at Jackson "with a look of mingled hatred and contempt," then muttered "a horrid malediction" upon his murderer. Goodbread collapsed into the street and died within moments.

"Is there any more damned rascals of Goodbread in town?" challenged Jackson. "If not, bring Alfred George, your sheriff." Jackson surrendered, and several of his friends signed the modest $200 bond. Released before Goodbread's body was cold, Jackson returned home,where a number of friends stood guard through the night.

Joseph Goodbread was the first victim of what would become the Regulator-Moderator War, and Mrs. Goodbread became the first widow. Charles Jackson organized a band of "Regulators" to take action against other criminals – and to protect himself from retribution.  Goodbread's friends pursued vengeance, organizing themselves into "Moderators" to "moderate" the Regulators. During the next four years more than thirty men who labeled themselves Regulators or Moderators were killed in ambushes, lynchings, assassinations, and pitched battles. The Regulator-Moderator War, although strangely overlooked by historians and popular mythmakers, produced more casualties than any other blood feud in the long history of frontier strife. A thorough account of this East Texas conflict is overdue, along with an evaluation of its proper rank in the annals of extralegal violence.

•••

The Regulators and Moderators who plunged East Texas into a murderous orgy of shooting and lynching were following an extralegal tradition that extended into the American past for three-quarters of a century. Violence against British authority was commonplace in the colonies for several years prior to the American Revolution. The Boston Massacre (1770) and the Boston Tea Party (1773) were the most famous of scores of riots that began in the mid-1760s. In this atmosphere of unsanctioned violence, an outbreak of frontier crime in South Carolina triggered a response by angry citizens which launched the vigilante tradition in America. From 1767 through 1769, respectable citizens organized themselves as "Regulators" and tried troublemakers, flogging and expelling many undesirables. One outlaw gang was cornered, and sixteen members were slain.[8]

This successful Regulator movement inspired hundreds of similar actions during the remainder of the eighteenth century, throughout the nineteenth century, and into the twentieth century. Many Regulator groups were highly organized and operated on a comparatively large scale, while others banded spontaneously to deal swiftly with a single criminal. For a century these extralegal groups usually were called "Regulators," but by the late nineteenth century the customary term had become "vigilante."

Another term common to extralegal experiences was provided by Colonel Charles Lynch, a prominent citizen of Bedford County, Virginia (the town of Lynchburg was named for Colonel Lynch). By 1780, with the Revolution still raging, Bedford County had become a hotbed of outlawry. Leading citizens formed a court with Colonel Lynch sitting as presiding judge. Regular – if illegal – trails were held, with flogging as the common punishment. This court thereby dispensed "Lynch Law," although in time this term came to mean a far more lethal form of justice than flogging.[9]

During the eighteenth, nineteenth, and twentieth centuries, more than 6,000 men and a few women were executed by vigilante activities. In his authoritative study of violence in America, Richard Maxwell Brown described the development of "the ideology of vigilantism," which "gripped the minds and emotions of Americans." Brown concluded that "the vigilantes, knowing full well that their actions were illegal, felt obliged to legitimize their violence by expounding a philosophy of vigilantism." By the mid-1800s, "self-righteous vigilantes…were routinely invoking 'self-preservation' or 'self-protection' as the first principal of vigilantism." Brown quoted a resolution of Indiana vigilantes from 1858:

> We are believers in the doctrine of popular sovereignty; that the people of this country are the real legal sovereigns, and that whenever the laws, made by those to whom they have relegated their authority, are found inadequate to their protection, it is the right of the people to take the protection of their prosperity in their own hands, and deal with these villains according to their just desserts….[10]

Such sentiments were embraced vigorously by pioneers, and vigilantism flourished on the western frontier in the nineteenth century. The westward movement often outraced the establishments of courts, law officers, and even jails. Extralegal action was quicker and cheaper than any system of courts, judges, juries, attorneys, trials, appeals, and institutional punishment. Wherever lawlessness broke out, prominent citizens encouraged, organized, and usually led vigilante groups in establishing order. "A host of distinguished Americans – statesmen, politicians, capitalists, lawyers, judges, writers, and others – supported vigilantism by word or deed," stated Brown. Usually their support or participation was when they were younger men, leaders on the rise, "but in later life, they never repudiated their actions." Brown specifically listed two future presidents (Andrew Jackson and Theodore Roosevelt), five U.S. senators, and eight governors of states or territories who had participated in vigilantism.[11]

Certainly, in frontier East Texas, the westward movement extended beyond courts, law officers, and jails. Shelby County and surrounding areas were overrun by criminals and desperados, but the fledgling legal apparatus of the new counties and of the Republic of Texas could not yet cope with the lawlessness of this wilderness region. Following the murder of Joseph Goodbread and subsequent reprisals, East Texans readily resorted to Regulators and lynching and ambuscade. Dr. Ashcroft of Shelbyville recalled that the Texas Republic was "without adequate resources for its own support," yet it had to repel Mexican invasions and combat "hordes of wild and merciless savages." The Republic "was indeed utterly powerless to preserve the ascendancy of law and order." As a consequence, in East Texas "the lynch code with all its horrors and severities was adopted...."[12]

During the next four years East Texans embraced a tradition of extralegal violence that had existed for more than seven decades. The Regulator-Moderator War escalated this rough but accepted practice to a new level of intensity and bloodshed. Although this intensity would never again be equaled by feudists, the lack of legal consequences undoubtedly encouraged the continuation of the feuding tradition. How, then, did the Regulators and Moderators of East Texas, battling each other with single-shot weapons in a sparsely-settled wilderness, produce a uniquely homicidal feud?

# Neutral Ground

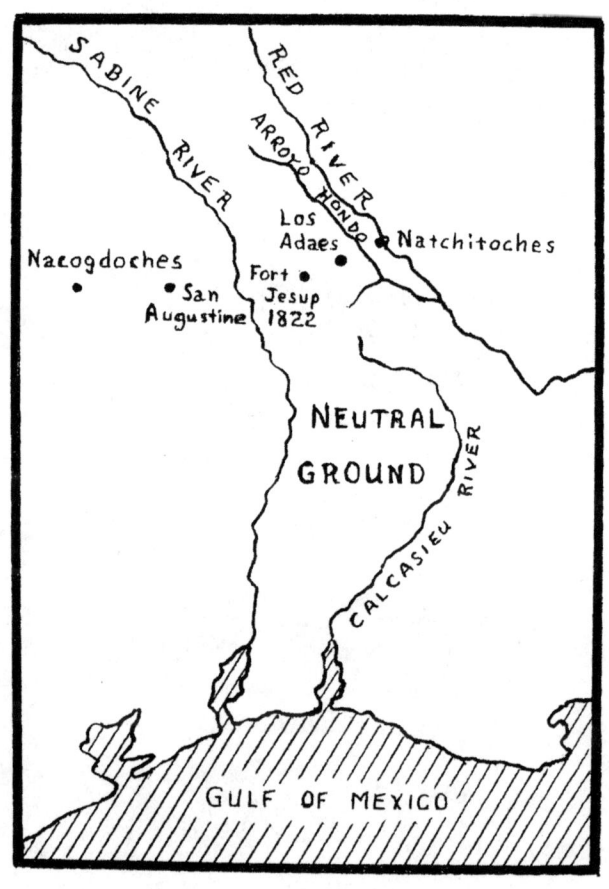

# 2 Regulator-Moderator Country

*"The man who had killed his man...was looked upon as a sort of gentleman; while a man who had stolen a horse or dealt in bogus money was universally detested."*
—Colonel Alexander Horton

An international development early in the nineteenth century influenced the Regulator-Moderator War. When Louisiana was transferred to the United States by the Louisiana Purchase of 1803, U.S. troops were stationed at Natchitoches, long a Spanish possession. The boundary of Texas was undetermined, and the Spanish countered by placing army contingents at Nacogdoches and at Los Adaes, only fifteen miles west of Natchitoches. Predictably, there were tensions between these nearby bands of opposing soldiers, and it seemed only a matter of time before shooting erupted.

To avert bloodshed and an international incident, the U.S. and Spanish commanders in Louisiana and Texas pragmatically decided to separate their troops in 1806 by declaring a Neutral Ground. Neither Spanish nor U.S. soldiers would be permitted to enter an area bounded by the Sabine River on the west, and, on the east, the Arroyo Hondo (a north-south creek located a few miles west of Natchitoches) and south to the Gulf of Mexico along the west bank of the Calcasieu River. This informal agreement kept peace between the two nations for a decade and a half. But with no military or other authority in effect, the Neutral Ground became a haven for fugitives from justice, ruffians, thieves, killers, and all manner of other criminals. Gangs of highwaymen preyed on travelers on *El Camino Real,* who had to form armed caravans to hope for safe passage.

In 1819 the Adams-Onis Treaty negotiated the Florida Purchase and, among other things, established a boundary between Texas and Louisiana. Although the Treaty was not ratified until 1821, scalawags and riffraff, by now firmly entrenched in an outlaw paradise, continued their nefarious activities. In 1822 Fort Jesup, a major U.S. military installation, was established alongside *El Camino Real* about twenty miles southwest of Natchitoches. Fort Jesup grew to a complex of eighty-two buildings, and troops stationed there worked to enforce law and order. But area rogues offered all manner of vice to off-duty soldiers. After one of his troopers was killed, Colonel Henry Leavenworth angrily denounced the perpetrators as, "Sticky-fingered, whiskey-selling, slave-stealing squatters."[1]

During the 1820s and 1830s, thousands of land-hungry emigrants passed the fort on their way to Texas. Passage was safer then, thanks to the efforts of the army. Hounded by the military,

Only remaining building of eighty-two structures which made up Fort Jesup. This kitchen and mess hall stood behind a two-story company barracks. *(Photo by Karon O'Neal)*

many of the fugitives and hooligans of the old Neutral Strip drifted into the unpoliced wilderness of East Texas. When settlers arrived to take possession of East Texas land grants, they soon learned about their unsavory neighbors. Although the Neutral Ground ceased to exist two decades before the Regulators and Moderators started killing each other, the outlawry it hosted stubbornly persisted and spread into Mexican Texas. By the time the Republic of Texas began dispersing large land grants, the criminal element in East Texas included land pirates, counterfeiters, murderers, slave stealers, horse thieves, fugitives from U.S. justice, and violent thugs.

There was a curious pecking order among this criminal aggregation, comparable to the informal alignment of inmates in a prison. "The one class were men who had killed their man or men, and were frequently gamblers," observed Colonel Alexander Horton. Horton had lived near San Augustine since 1824, served General Sam Houston as aide-de-camp, and fought at the Battle of San Jacinto. A long career in public service included tenures as sheriff of San Augustine County, and he would be called upon to subdue hostilities between Regulators and Moderators. "The other class were men who dealt in horses without buying, and in bogus money…. There was no congeniality between these two classes of men," reflected Horton. "The man-killer and gambler detested the man who traded in stolen horses and bogus money. The man who had killed his man, even without a cause, was looked upon as a sort of gentleman; while a man who had stolen a horse or dealt in bogus money was universally destested."[2]

Nacogdoches and San Augustine, older communities which usually attracted honest, ambitious settlers, pressured their worst lawbreakers into moving elsewhere. Many unruly criminals drifted north into what became Shelby County. "Unlike her sister counties," observed *The Redlander* of San Augustine, after the Regulator-Moderator War had begun, "Shelby has failed to get rid of a redundant and vicious portion of her citizens, who, being first to establish there, have succeeded so far, in maintaining their position…." *The Redlander* pointed out that it was common knowledge "that a band of outlaws and murderers have infested that county or a portion of it, since its first settlement." While the population of Shelby County "has increased rapidly in recent years," the better class of citizens "have waited in vain for a change." Indeed, Shelby County had attained a "notoriety abroad as a place of refuge for felons...."[3]

One Shelby County felon was Captain Charles Jackson, killer, and another was Joseph Goodbread, land pirate. Apparently the class distinction described by Alexander Horton was at work between these two men. As a former riverboat captain who had killed his man, Jackson looked down upon the swindler Goodbread. Like a haughty gentleman of the era who felt free to cane his inferiors, Captain Jackson did not hesitate to shoot down the disreputable Goodbread.

After Goodbread was murdered, Shelby County was torn by so much bloodshed that the conflict became known as "The Shelby County War." But violent events, along with Regulator and Moderator organizations, already had begun in Harrison County, and soon would spread into Panola District and other counties. "The Regulator-Moderator War" provides a more comprehensive label.

Shelby County was organized in 1836 by the Congress of the Republic of Texas from the old Tenehaw Municipality of Mexican Texas. Named for Isaac Shelby, American Revolutionary soldier and the first governor of Kentucky, the county seat was the village of Nashville, soon renamed Shelbyville. The sparsely-settled county stretched far to the north, and in 1839 Harrison County was created from the northern reaches of Shelby County. Two years later plantation owner Peter Whetstone donated land for a county seat, which was named Marshall. The wilderness area between Harrison and Shelby counties was Panola District (Panola County was not organized until 1846). The seat of government was the log cabin hamlet Pulaski, located on the Sabine River, which served as temporary county seat for Harrison County prior to the organization of Marshall. San Augustine began as a Mexican village on *El Camino Real,* and San Augustine County was an original county of the Texas Republic.

The great attraction of this region and the rest of early Texas was land – lots of land, in tracts of a size that settlers could not hope to acquire in the United States. By the Land Act of 1820, the U.S. government would sell eighty acres of western land to a settler for $100. Just five years later the Mexican government, having decided to attract Anglo farmers to the province of Texas, enacted a Colonization Law which offered a league of land (4,428 acres) to a stock raiser, and a *labor* (177 acres) to a farmer. Most Anglos called themselves stock farmers and acquired both a league and a *labor* (4,605 acres). Fees, which could be paid out over a period of years – and in practice sometimes were not paid at all – totaled less than $100, a smaller price than a mere eighty acres on the U.S. frontier.

The Texas Constitution of 1836 allowed everyone who already held land to keep it. The Republic soon passed a law permitting all heads of families who were living in Texas on March 2, 1836, to receive a league and a labor of land, while all single men could claim one-third of a league (1,476 acres). In 1837, President Sam Houston's administration provided for the surveying of public lands into sections of 640 acres each (one mile by one mile), and new Texas settlers began acquiring 640-acre tracts.

Whether the settler's headright was 4,428 acres or 1,476 acres, or even 640 acres, a farmer – even with the help of sons – could clear and cultivate only a relatively few acres of East Texas virgin timberland. East Texas settlers lived on subsistence farms in log cabins, raised a few hogs and made almost everything they used. Little cash or coin circulated and most transactions were by barter. Josiah Gregg, who traveled through East Texas in 1841, observed that most settlers, "being of backwoods raising,…live in the plainest and worst style."[4] But men who came to Texas had a passion for land – the more the better, even if they could not cultivate much of it.

Pioneer settlers willingly accepted hardships and dangers to acquire their own land, and were unlikely to be intimidated by the criminal riffraff who gravitated to the East Texas wilderness. Settlers regarded land swindlers as the most despicable of villains – land title forgers, as they were known, or land counterfeiters, or, of course, land pirates. Whatever they were called, to land-hungry East Texans they were as intolerable as claim-jumpers to miners, or rustlers to cattle ranchers.

Most frontiersmen were descended from pioneer families. Pioneer children grew up learning to hunt and cook and work in the fields. They became familiar with Indian alarms and other frontier hazards. Despite the isolation of frontier life, they understood group effort, from log rollings to quilting bees to rallying against common enemies. When they grew into men and women, they possessed the skills and temperament to advance to the next frontier – particularly if that frontier offered vast tracts of land. Such people understood that life would be hard on the edge of settlement, but the deeded prize was worth peril and back-breaking labor. They were prepared to overcome the obstacles of nature or of hostile warriors – or of nearby criminals. They knew that sometimes it was necessary for men to ride in pursuit of war parties, and they understood the tradition of banding together as Regulators against lawlessness. Josiah Gregg remarked upon this lawlessness and the resulting "lynchings and outraged citizens."[5]

East Texas frontiersmen comprised an armed society, and two significant developments in weapons impacted the ordnance of the Regulator-Moderator War. The standard weapon employed by

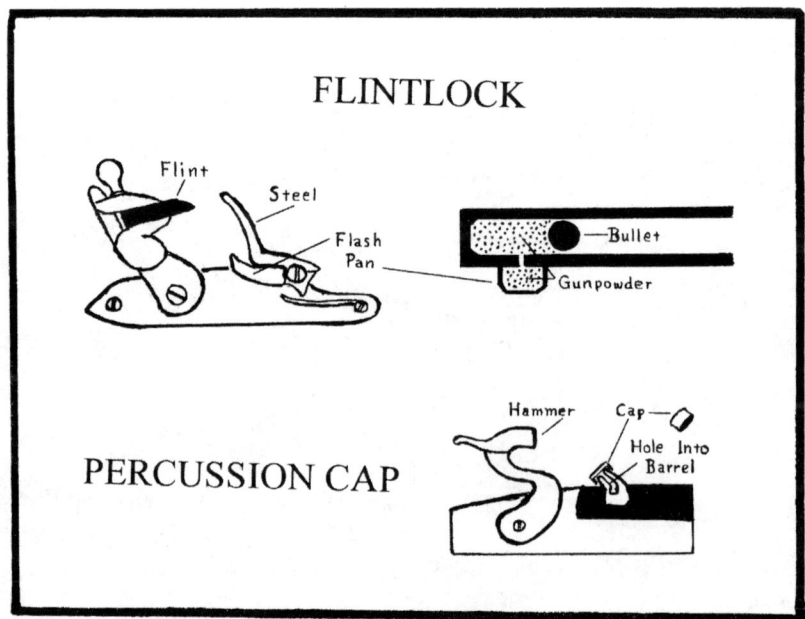

FLINTLOCK

Flint
Steel
Flash Pan
Bullet
Gunpowder

PERCUSSION CAP

Hammer
Cap
Hole Into Barrel

most Regulators and Moderators was one version or another of the Kentucky long rifle. Long-barreled "Kentucky" flintlock rifles were developed in the mid-1700s by Pennsylvania gunsmiths, then used by Daniel Boone and other pioneers on the Kentucky frontier. Accurate at 150 or even 200 yards, the Kentucky rifle became the primary weapon for generations of frontiersmen.[6]

The first U.S. patents for percussion firearms were filed in the early 1820s, and long rifles were improved by a superior ignition system. The old flintlock system required flint and frizzen to ignite a splash of powder in an exterior flashpan, which would explode the main powder charge inside the barrel. But the powder in the flashpan might not ignite because of loose flints or damp weather, a frequent condition in East Texas. With fighting imminent between East Texas feudists, M.T. Johnson exhorted his fellow Regulators to "lick your flints [and] keep your powder dry...."[7] When the trigger was pulled on a flintlock, aim had to be maintained, because it took an instant for the dual ignition.

Beginning in the 1820s, fulminate of mercury was enclosed in a copper percussion cap, which was placed over a nipple opening into the base of the barrel and the powder charge. After cocking the hammer, a pull of the trigger dropped the hammer onto the cap, and the gun discharged instantly without the split-second delay of the flintlock. A man who was not an expert marksman stood a far better chance of hitting a moving target with a percussion rifle than with a flintlock. And even in a rain the percussion cap was reliable, unlike the powder in the flashpan of a wet flintlock.

The advantages were obvious, and flintlocks could be converted to percussion cap ignition by any gunsmith. By the time of the Regulator-Moderator War, percussion rifles – either conversions or new models – were common among frontiersmen. Even the U.S. Army, notoriously slow in the nineteenth century to embrace new weaponry, adapted a percussion arm in 1841. Despite the new innovation, a number of East Texas frontiersmen continued to rely on their old-fashioned flintlocks.

Whether flintlock or percussion, the long rifles often were equipped with double-set triggers. After the first trigger was set, the remaining trigger fired the gun with the slightest pressure. There

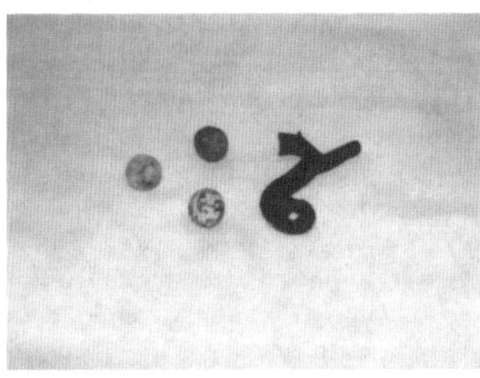

Three .58 caliber rifle balls and a percussion cap rifle hammer. These and other artifacts were found by Johnny Hargrove near the Hargrove home at the site of the final battle. (Photo by the author)

would be no hard pull of the trigger finger to move the barrel and spoil marksmanship. An increasing number of rifles were double-barreled, either over-and-under or side-by-side, thereby doubling the firepower before reloading was necessary. Many East Texans were expert arms handlers who could fire two or three aimed shots per minute from a single-shot rifle.

Percussion caps were purchased and carried in a pocket or in a container which could facilitate replacement on a nipple. Rifle balls also could be purchased, but many men preferred to mold their own ammunition since the slightest imperfection could send the bullet off-target. One-pound bars of lead were used, and ammunition calibers were large. Fifty bullets to the pound, for instance, produced .45 caliber balls; forty bullets to the pound were in .49 caliber; thirty bullets to the pound were .51 caliber; thirty-five bullets to the pound were .54 caliber; and twenty-four balls to the pound were .57 caliber. These were common calibers, and such large bullets created ghastly injuries. Soft lead balls flatten upon contact with tissue, inflicting lethal internal wounds. Even when such ammunition strikes a limb, the effect is to splinter a bone, rather than to create a clean break that might heal. Medical treatment in East Texas still was primitive, and Regulators and Moderators struck by large-caliber lead balls had rather bleak prospects of recovery.

Single-shot pistols also were produced in large calibers, and many handguns had two barrels so they could be fired twice before reloading. Moderator Henry Strickland carried a Derringer,[8] a short-barreled pistol popular as a hideout gun. When Regulators and

Moderators were mounted, they carried a loaded rifle across the saddle pommel, and often a pistol or two in saddle holsters.

A revolutionary new handgun was obtained by a few East Texans. In 1836, young Samuel Colt began manufacturing his new invention, revolving pistols, in Paterson, New Jersey. The Paterson Colt held five bullets, available in .28, .31, and .36 calibers. In six years Colt produced 2,850 revolving pistols and 1,912 revolving rifles and shotguns. But the small-caliber Colt revolver was difficult to reload, and with limited demand, the factory in Paterson closed in 1842. Texans appreciated a repeating handgun, and the Texas Republic had ordered 180 Paterson revolvers. Armed with two five-shooters apiece, Texas Rangers could successfully battle mounted Comanche warriors, and in 1847 a far larger wartime order put Sam Colt back into business. In the meantime, a few early Paterson Colts made their way into the hands of Regulators and Moderators, although these innovative weapons exerted little impact on the hostilities.

Perhaps there were a few Colt revolving rifles on the Regulator-Moderator front, and certainly there were numerous double-barreled shotguns. These lethal weapons, loaded with buckshot, often were carried by horsemen. Robert Potter even had a small artillery piece at his cabin on Caddo Lake, as well as an impressive arsenal of other weapons. When Regulators surrounded his cabin, his common-law wife, Harriet Page, pleaded with Potter to mount a defense. "We had a cannon and plenty of firearms, all loaded, and I reminded him that I could load guns as fast as he

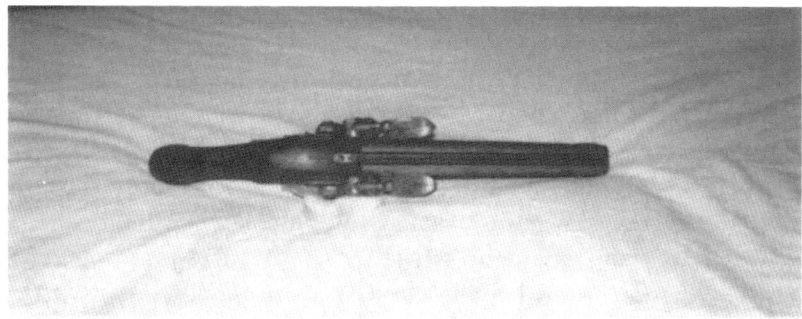

Double-barreled flintlock pistol. *(Photo by the author)*

could."[9] A great many East Texas women could handle firearms, and so could their children. Boys on every frontier were given guns and taught to shoot at about the age of seven. Their first gun usually was a short-barreled rifle, handed down to a little brother as the older sibling grew into a full-size firearm.

Virtually every man in East Texas hunted wild game. These hunters cleaned and butchered their kills, often aided by wives and children. East Texas farm families also butchered their own hogs. Through such day-to-day activities East Texans became accustomed to the sight of blood and to the death of animals. Such people were not squeamish, and when Regulators and Moderators began shooting at each other, most East Texans faced the growing bloodshed with hardened fortitude.

Warlike resolve was not confined to men. Harriet Page urged Robert Potter to fight, and she certainly was not the only woman in East Texas who "could load guns as fast as he could." Like other East Texas women, Harriet often was left alone – except for the children – while her common-law husband was away, and she became "quite a woodsman."[10] Charles Jackson's wife seemed to harbor no deep regrets that he had been compelled to kill "rascals," and she exhorted him "to kill a few more...."[11] Throughout the Regulator-Moderator War, wives on both sides rode horseback through the wilds of Shelby County in the role of scout. "We had ladies out all the time acting as spies for us, watching the movements of the moderators," related John W. Middleton.[12] Middleton listed four women, including Helen Daggett Moorman, who would play an especially daring role. Other women unflinchingly bandaged and nursed their wounded husbands.

A common phrase heard in Shelby County suggested that a man did or did not "know when the deer fed." Newcomers thought it was a hunter's phrase or, according to Eph Daggett, "that I was an ignoramus, foolish, etc." But after Daggett earned their respect he was told the local meaning: "Men who 'knew when the deer fed' were reliable and could be trusted...."[13] A corresponding term developed some years later in the last West, when a trustworthy man would "do to ride the river with." The unrestrained criminal element and well-armed, land-hungry settlers produced a volatile mix in East Texas. During the ensuing four years of warfare, a great many men and women, Regulators and Moderators, proved that they "knew when the deer fed." Although some settlers moved away from the scene of violence, most East Texas pioneers stubbornly and courageously stood their ground, taking up arms to defend their homes and friends.

Milton Garrett built this cabin of squared logs in 1826 (ten miles west of San Augustine)on the south side of *El Camino Real*. The oldest log cabin in Texas is divided into two rooms, and a thirty-foot-long sleeping loft is beneath the roof.

# 3 Jackson's Regulators

*"I'd rather be hung than whipped to death."*
—Squire Humphries, horse thief

After shooting Joseph Goodbread in cold blood, almost immediately Charles Jackson was released on bond. On April 29, 1841, a bill of indictment was handed down: "That Charles W. Jackson...without the fear of God before his eyes but moved and actuated by the devil, did, with a rifle of the value of $20.00, loaded with powder and ball, shoot Joseph Goodbread thereby killing him."[1]

Jackson became "somewhat alarmed at the formidable preparations made to convict him by the prosecuting attorney," according to Shelbyville physician Levi Ashcroft. A change of venue to Harrison County was secured, and the trial would take place two months later in Pulaski, the temporary county seat. Judge Thomas Johnson refused bail and ordered Jackson jailed. Sheriff Alfred George responded that the jail was in disrepair and that he would place a guard over the prisoner. "But no sooner had court adjourned, and the judge gotten clearly out of sight," related Dr. Ashcroft, "than the sheriff turned his charge loose...."[2]

Jackson twice had attained almost immediate release from the custody of Sheriff George, a clear indication that the legal machinery of Shelby County exercised little real authority. Although this laxity worked to his advantage, Jackson understood that the general lawlessness placed him in danger from Goodbread's fellow criminals who wanted revenge. But Jackson also recognized opportunity in the legal anarchy in Shelby County. Sheriff George was not the only citizen who regarded the death of Goodbread as

Horse thieves fired a bullet through the front door of the Milton Garrett cabin. *(Photo by the author)*

good riddance. The country swarmed with other criminals, and Jackson worked to institute the tradition of Regulators into Shelby County.

"Chance favored him," remarked Dr. Ashcroft, who deeply disliked Jackson. "About this time quite a large number of cattle were stolen from various persons in the neighborhood, and, for the ostensible purpose of punishing the marauders, Jackson set about the organization of a company of marauders."[3]

Livestock theft and violence were nothing new in East Texas. Horse thieves had run rampant for years, riding in gangs and sometimes boldly taking the mount of a solitary rider on a public road. A band of horse thieves, riding on *El Camino Real* about ten miles west of San Augustine, for some reason fired at the cabin of Milton Garrett. One bullet pierced the door and plowed into an interior wall.[4] In 1837 a gang member named Anderson was guarding "a large number of horses with their bridles and saddles" in an open field about four miles east of Shelbyville. The horses had been stolen in Louisiana, and when pursuers located their animals, they killed Anderson.[5]

Soon after migrating from North Carolina to Shelbyville in 1836, Dr. Ashcroft lost one of his carriage horses to a neighbor, Major Thomas Bell. After his horse vanished, Dr. Ashcroft threatened Bell and filed suit in court, to no avail. Dr. Ashcroft noticed that a Shelby County "clan," or gang of criminals, was large enough to control local elections, which then allowed them to escape prosecution, or jail, or conviction. Particularly odious to Dr. Ashcroft was a lanky justice of the peace named Jonas Phelps, who wore a coonskin cap in his tiny courtroom. "He was too lazy and indolent to be an active member of the clan," but Judge Phelps used his official position to aid Shelby County's "rascaldom."[6]

Prior to the organization of the Regulators in Shelby County, exasperated settlers sometimes rose up spontaneously against criminals, which prepared them for a more systematic means of regulating. In 1838, a Shelby County pursuit party trailed stolen horses to the cabin and corrals of A.F. Brown. Brown was bound, hauled into Shelbyville, then publicly lynched in the original manner, by flogging. Dr. Ashcroft reported that "he was entirely denuded of his clothes, tied to a tree and whipped until his back wore the appearance of a raw beefsteak." The grass and leaves beneath his feet became clotted with blood, noted Dr. Ashcroft, "yet the blows ceased not; stripe after stripe fell upon his bare and bleeding back, thick, fast and furious; -- the lynchers taking the whip by turns as one would become exhausted...." Later someone carved on the whipping tree: "A.F. Brown, for horsestealing."[7]

That same year about twenty armed men rode to the home of a horse thief named Beauchamp, located a few miles east of Shelbyville. The rustler hid in the woods, but the posse informed Mrs. Beauchamp "that he should leave the country within twenty

Interior-view reveals sunlight through the bullet hole, and the hole where the ball entered the dividing wall. *(Photo by the author)*

four hours or receive one hundred lashes on his bare back." Within a short time Beauchamp departed for Arkansas, leaving his wife and children to fend for themselves. In Arkansas, Beauchamp took up with another woman, while Mrs. Beauchamp remarried and moved west. Flogging was not confined to horse thieves. A land buyer was robbed of $1,700 by Willis Watson, a notorious counterfeiter and thief, and an accomplice named Mordecai at a San Augustine tavern. "The men were arrested and whipped every day until a confession was obtained," stated John Middleton. Watson ran a ferry on the Sabine River that "was the headquarters of counterfeiters and desperate characters" – until angry citizens burned him out in 1838.[8]

So for two or three years, East Texans occasionally banded together to take harsh action against the most outrageous evildoers in their area. Charles Jackson then organized this regulator impulse against the abundance of outlaws in Shelby County. Jackson was under indictment for murder and needed to improve his image, and a body of armed Regulators could offer protection against the dangerous men who wanted revenge for the death of Joseph Goodbread. Charles Jackson, known to have killed other men in at least two encounters, commanded respect from a society in which self-defense was an admirable attribute. He attracted friends who signed his bond and guarded his home after the Goodbread killing, and he was confident that men would serve under him as Regulators. Although Dr. Ashcroft scorned Jackson as selfish, cowardly, and "a notorious desperado," he grudgingly conceded that "he was eminently suited to become the leader of a lawless mob."[9]

Jackson hosted "a public dinner" at which he organized men to regulate lawbreakers and to uncover stolen property. John Middleton reported that "a company of sixty-three men was made and a day appointed for the meeting of the company, but only twenty-three men came and they went in pursuit." Jackson's friend Eph Daggett said that there were fourteen riders, while Dr. Ashcroft thought there were "about thirty men, mostly restless and desperate characters, who had nothing to lose but their lives, which were only valuable to themselves."[10]

Jackson and his first band of Regulators, whether fourteen or twenty-three or thirty in number, pursued and captured a trio of stock thieves who had stolen about thirty horses. The Regulators seized Squire Humphries, who held an isolated headright in northwestern Shelby County; his brother-in-law, a young man named West; and West's father. Jackson's extralegal posse then "took off Humphries' shirt, tied him lengthwise on a tanning log, and whipped his back unmercifully." When Humphries refused to confess, he was turned over, and "an old Red River overseer" began whipping him near the chin. Pointing to Humphries' stomach, his tormentor said, "When I get to his belly he'll belch the truth."[11]

"Let me up," shouted Humphries. "I am guilty and will let the whole truth come. I don't want to be abused any more. I'd rather be hung than whipped to death."

During the ensuing confession, Humphries pointed out that one of his earliest memories of boyhood was of holding stolen horses. "I was raised to do these things."

The senior West admitted that he had served as instructor of horse thievery and that his son and Humphries simply were obeying orders. "I am ready to undergo anything," he pleaded, "but spare my son."

After a long consultation, the two younger men were released and told to leave the country. West was detained, and Jackson and his men tried to import attorney Thomas J. Rusk from Nacogdoches "to appear for the Regulators to the indictment." But this attempt at legal prosecution failed, "as the court was broken up." With anarchy reigning in Shelby County, district court did not meet for the next four years.

Jackson, at the head of armed riders, decided to launch a pre-emptive strike against two sets of brothers, the Stricklands and the McFaddens, desperados who lived with their families near the line of Panola District and Shelby County. These dangerous men had been friends with Joseph Goodbread, and Jackson "could never feel himself safe so long as they remained in the country...."[12]

Anyone was unsafe who incurred the enmity of the Strickland and McFadden brothers. In 1838 Jim Strickland, the "Tiger of the Tenehaw," was riding a stolen mare which was recognized by Ben Odell, who informed Henry Cannon, owner of the horse. Tiger Jim threatened Odell's life, and angrily released the mare, which returned to Cannon's place. At a dinner and dance in Shelbyville, Tiger Jim and Odell were on the dance floor at the same time. John Middleton reported that the two men "intended shooting as they passed" and pressed the muzzles of their pistols against each other. Odell's gun misfired, but Strickland triggered a round point-blank. Although Odell gamely knocked Tiger Jim down with his fist, the wounded man died the next morning. At the next session of Shelby County's ineffectual district court, Strickland and three counterfeiters each won acquittal.[13]

In addition to being a killer and a horse thief, Tiger Jim Strickland also traded in stolen slaves. "Tiger Jim had a yellow complexion, and his countenance was without expression," described Eph Daggett. "He could not laugh, but made a curious noise when he affected to laugh." Nursing "a spite" against a settler, Strickland stole and butchered seven of the man's hogs and fired a load of buckshot at his cabin, wounding his stepson.[14]

After realizing that a surveyor named McClure had evidence against him for one of his misdeeds, Tiger Jim enlisted "Buckskin Bill" McFadden and rode to the Sabine River, where McClure boarded with a Mr. and Mrs. Kelly. While McClure worked at a table, two men rode up and shouted, "We have found the damned rascal." When they dismounted and leveled their rifles, Mrs. Kelly bravely came out "and told them that they were ruffians and had better go home and make something to feed their starving little ones." Ignoring Mrs. Kelly, the ruffians fired and instantly killed McClure. "They then defied the law and resisted arrest," related John Middleton.[15]

Tiger Jim Strickland's brother, Henry, was "one of the most ferocious men I ever knew," stated Eph Daggett. "Henry had been the bully of the Tenaha for a long time," although he was carved up badly in a knife fight by "Riproaring Jim" Forsythe. Daggett told of another encounter when Henry was stabbed in the chest with "an old rusty dirk," and soon developed a fever and began to spit blood. Daggett found Henry and nursed him with the rough and ready home remedies commonly administered to Regulators and Moderators. "I got from my private medicine box rhubarb and alum, took some padding and screwed it into the hole, made a large slippery elm poultice that went all around his body, kept his bowels regular and dieted him. I cooked his food, pulled him through in ten days and had him on his feet again." Although described as "skinny,"

Henry obviously had a strong constitution. He was dark, "had a vicious eye, and was domineering in his appearance."[16]

The Strickland brothers often hid out in the canebrakes and forests of Shelby County and Panola District. They waylaid travelers, sometimes using Squire Humphries as an accomplice. Other confederates of the Stricklands were the McFadden brothers, Bill, John, and fourteen-year-old Baily, who was serving his rogue's apprenticeship. "They were bad men, doubtless," asserted Dr. Ashcroft.[17]

Such incorrigible criminals were obvious targets of a Regulator group attempting to rid the countryside of lawbreakers. It is not known if Jackson intended to resort to flogging again, or if Regulator justice would have escalated to executing the Stricklands and McFaddens. When Jackson and his men rode up to the Strickland home, both Tiger Jim and Henry were absent. Jackson posted a guard detail around the cabin, so that Tiger Jim's wife could not leave to sound the alarm.[18]

Jackson and the rest of his men rode on to the McFadden place, but these brothers also were gone. After holding "a council of war," the Regulators decided to burn the houses. Despite "the screams and entreaties of the women and children," the McFadden dwellings were set on fire. With these cabins reduced to ashes, the Regulators rode back to the Strickland home and set it ablaze.

When the brothers returned to their burned cabins and to their homeless wives and children, they were filled with rage. And with the murderous resolve of hardened criminals, "they swore a solemn oath of vengeance...."

A couple of months after this incendiary expedition, the Harrison County district court convened in Pulaski in July 1841. The log structures of the village occupied a rough triangle on a bluff overlooking the Sabine River. Pulaski was located on the east bank of the Sabine. Just north of the hamlet a road led to the river ferry.

The presiding judge was John M. Hansford, a native of Kentucky who, in the late 1830s, established a home in Jonesville in the eastern portion of Shelby County – a portion which later became part of Harrison County. In 1838 Hansford won election to the House of Representatives of the Third Congress of the Republic of Texas, and he became speaker of the House. The next year, he was re-elected to the Fourth Congress. On January 31, 1840, he was appointed judge of the Seventh District Court. In July 1841, Judge Hansford rode south to Pulaski and made camp just outside of town, since there was no tavern or stable.[19]

Sheriff Alfred George "summoned twenty men from the ranks of Capt. Jackson's company to guard the prisoner...." There were expectations of assassination attempts, and Jackson apparently intended to use his bodyguards to intimidate the court – just as he had the Shelby County court. The twenty guards were "armed with double barreled shot guns, knives and pistols," and a large number of other Regulators also made their way to Pulaski. It was rumored that several of Jackson's enemies also came to Pulaski and that Tiger Jim Strickland had established a sniper's position in a cornfield on the outskirts of town. There was a search for Strickland, but he was not found, and there were no attempts on Jackson's life.[20]

On Friday, July 16, 1841, Judge Hansford convened the court. The one-room log courthouse was crowded with armed men, including Jackson. Judge Hansford fined Harrison County Sheriff Hugh Pope for permitting a prisoner to bring weapons into court,

Looking north at the Sabine River from the bluff occupied by Pulaski. A wagon road at right went down to the east bank and a ferry. *(Photo by the author)*

and Jackson then placed his weapons on the judicial bench. It was a hot day, so Jackson arrogantly removed his coat and shoes and demanded his trial. Judge Hansford dealt with the preliminaries of the trial, then spent the rest of the day seating a jury -- James Asher, Young Bates, James Booker, Frederick Cox, James Daugherty, John Gibbs, Francis Jordan, Jackson LaGrone, Markes Mates, W.A. Pope, E.M. Reese, and Elijah Williams. Hansford adjourned court until the next morning at nine o'clock.[21]

Judge Hansford retired to his camp, shaken by the presence of Jackson's heavily armed men. Regulator and Moderator groups already had been organized in Harrison County. A trio of related killings included the brazen assassination by Regulators of the county sheriff earlier in the year. Now a band of Shelby County Regulators, bristling with shotguns and pistols, established themselves in Hansford's courtroom. While digesting this grim development, during the evening he learned "that it would not be safe for him to proceed with the trial." The judge cowered at the prospect of putting his life on the line for law and order. Deciding to desert the legal battlefield under cover of darkness, Judge Hansford wrote these instructions to the sheriff and court clerk:[22]

To the Sheriff of Harrison County, Texas.

Being unwilling to risk my person in the court house any longer, when I see myself surrounded by bravos and hired assassins, and no longer free to preside as an impartial judge at the special term of the court called for the trial of Charles W. Jackson, I order you to adjourn court tomorrow at eight o'clock, by proclamation of this day.

From your hands at the regular time, I shall expect the prisoner. You will receive the prisoner and keep him safely, thereby causing him to be securely ironed and keeping a strong guard until delivered by due course of law.

Yours, etc.

*John H. Hansford*

Judge of the Seventh Judicial District

Having assigned Sheriff Pope the dangerous task of placing Jackson in irons, Judge Hansford provided permission for the court clerk, Samuel Stinson, to follow his example and retreat from Pulaski:[23]

> To the Clerk of the District Court,
> Harrison County, Texas.
>
> Sire, the gradual development of circumstances which have come to my knowledge since and before the commencement of the special trial of the District Court, and more particularly this evening, have assumed such a character that the District Judge is no longer free in the exercise of his functions as the presiding officer of the court, and unwilling to act as such any longer unless he can choose without compulsion or restraint, he is determined to avoid the mockery of holding a court under the government and control of hired assassins and to refuse the safety of his person to meet the menace without sufficient force for his protection.
>
> You will preserve with care the records, and consider yourself no longer bound to attend court at Pulaski, the county seat.
>
> I have the honor to be yours and etc.
> *John M. Hansford*
> Judge of the Seventh Judicial District

Judge Hansford arranged for the delivery of these documents, then disappeared into the night. His craven behavior in Pulaski, coupled with drunken appearances on the bench and rumors that he was a land counterfeiter, resulted in impeachment proceedings by the Congress of the Republic of Texas. On January 19, 1842, Hansford resigned his judgeship and the articles of impeachment were withdrawn. But at his home in Harrison County, Hansford again would find himself confronted by the mortal danger he had fled in Pulaski.

On Saturday morning, July 17, 1841, an expectant crowd

packed the little courtroom in Pulaski. The jury, the district attorney, and counsel for the defense were present. Charles Jackson was there, and so were the Regulators. At mid-morning, Sheriff Pope announced that Judge Hansford had departed and that the trial would be postponed. But defense counsel – perhaps already aware that Hansford had deserted his courtroom – persuaded the jury to hear the case. The jury announced "that they had been sworn to try the case, and whether the judge came or not they intended to do it." Although District Attorney H.P. Brewster was invited to present testimony, he wisely declined. The defense counsel addressed the jury, emphasizing the right of self-defense – and presumably did not mention that the victim was unarmed. A request for acquittal was granted by the jury.[24]

With at least twenty – and probably many more – armed Regulators in Pulaski, it was impossible for Sheriff Pope to arrest Jackson and place him in irons. The Regulator captain walked out of the Pulaski courthouse with his friends. With the retreat of Judge Hansford and the ensuing farce of a trial, the district court of Harrison County seemed as ineffective as the Shelby County district court, which further emboldened Regulators and their Moderator counterparts.

Charles Jackson arrogantly marched his Regulators from Pulaski into Harrison County and arrested Samuel McHenry, judge of the probate court. Jackson had learned that a $250 reward had been posted in Louisiana for McHenry because he had stolen slaves and brought them to Natchitoches. The Regulators collected their reward, and McHenry was sentenced to seven years in prison. Jackson and his Regulators rounded up several more slave stealers for delivery to Natchitoches in anticipation of receiving the same reward. "That was a money making business," remarked one Regulator.[25]

Watt Moorman led the Regulator movement in Shelby County. He was ruthless but capable of great charm. Moorman carried a brace of pistols, a bowie knife, a heavy bois d'arc stick, and a hunting horn to signal his men. *(Courtesy Shelby County Historical Museum)*

# 4 Watt Moorman

*"Jackson had but few friends, and they were
not such as to be much affected by his death."*
—Dr. Levi Ashcroft

The Stricklands and McFaddens and their fellow desperados decided to retaliate against Charles Jackson and the Regulators. The outlaw brothers, like other area criminals, hid out in the woods, keeping themselves concealed from law officers, angry victims, or other enemies. But Charles Jackson had committed murder on a public street, and evaded legal consequences for his action. With his armed Regulators, Jackson launched a harsh campaign against prominent felons. Acting as an arm of justice, if not of the law, Regulators administered floggings and burned the homes of "Freebooters." The legal machinery of Shelby County virtually ceased to exist. Sheriff Alfred George, "fearing danger to his life," fled to Nacogdoches for "two or three months" and appointed John Middleton as deputy sheriff.[1]

Shelby County's "Freebooters" were not the kind of men to remain targets for long. Ruthless and dangerous, they yearned for revenge against these law-and-order pretenders who had left their wives and children homeless. With no law enforcement to worry about, they decided to organize another company of riders and dispense their own justice.

Thirty or more men met and elected Edward Merchant their commander. Merchant had fled to Texas after killing a man in

Alabama, which had earned him grudging respect from rough men in a wild land. "Merchant was a man of undoubted courage, and determination of character," observed Dr. Ashcroft. A man known as Judge Hawkins suggested the label "Moderators," and the company drew up a code of regulations. The Moderators declared that the turmoil of the country had caused them to organize, "and they pledged themselves to sustain the legal tribunals in all efforts to punish the guilty and maintain order and tranquility."[2]

The first effort by the Moderators to "maintain order and tranquility" was to assassinate Charles W. Jackson. The eager volunteers were Tiger Jim and Henry Strickland, Bill, John and fourteen-year-old Baily McFadden, and Squire Humphries. The Stricklands and McFaddens, of course, had their homes burned by Jackson and his Regulators, who had flogged Squire Humphries viciously. Jackson had inflicted other wounds that demanded blood for retribution. Two other desperados named Bledsoe and Boatright also rode on the mission.[3]

A youngster named Choate informed the Moderators when Jackson traveled to Logansport on business, unaccompanied by his Regulators. His only companion was "a simple-minded, unoffending Dutchman named Lour," a grocery clerk in Shelbyville. Jackson reached Logansport safely but an ambush was set for his return trip. The unimproved public roads of Shelby County were little more than narrow trails through the forests – ideal for the concealment of assassins. Armed with shotguns, the Moderators dispersed into three positions where the road penetrated a dense thicket. Jackson and Lour appeared, and the hidden gunmen loosed a volley at point-blank range, "literally filling their bodies with buckshot." Jackson was blasted out of the saddle, dead before he reached the ground. Lour was still alive. He was taken to the nearest house and died the next morning.[4]

The murder of Lour, according to Dr. Ashcroft, "engendered a spirit of indignation in the breast of many of the best citizens of the county and induced them to take sides with the Regulators." While the death of Charles Jackson caused little remorse, the assassins realized that "it would be extremely hazardous for them to remain in the country." But the Moderators were energized by their coup against the Regulators, and fifty-five men guarded the McFadden place while the killers prepared to flee westward. The McFaddens took their families with them, and the Moderator company accompanied them "beyond the point of danger...."[5]

Deputy Sheriff John Middleton was not intimidated. A native of North Carolina, Middleton had moved his family to Shelby County in 1838. In 1841 he was thirty-eight years of age, and a veteran of Indian campaigning for the Republic of Texas. Deputy Middleton recruited eight men to ride with him in pursuit: Watt Moorman, who had helped to burn the Strickland and McFadden cabins; Frank and Monroe Hooper; Lee Truitt; Tom Josy; John Myrick; James Vaughan; and Sam Wallace. Middleton led his posse in "a circuitous route to avoid the clan." They crossed the Neches River and proceeded toward Crockett on *El Camino Real*.[6]

At some point the Moderator fugitives split up, and the posse followed the trail of Tiger Jim Strickland northward. Middleton and his men jumped Tiger Jim in his camp about twenty-five miles north of Crockett, near the residence of "One-Eyed" Williams. An old hand at eluding capture, Tiger Jim escaped into a thicket. The posse remained on guard through the night and heard sounds in the brush, but Strickland did not return to his camp. The next day, while Middleton and his men were eating at a house located near the camp, Tiger Jim and One-Eyed Williams blundered onto the scene. Spotting the posse members, they wheeled their horses. John Myrick's rifle shot struck Strickland in the shoulder. Strickland dropped his rifle but stayed on his horse. Clinging to the side of his mount like a Comanche warrior, Tiger Jim galloped away without further injury.[7]

In making yet another escape, Tiger Jim collided with One-Eyed Williams. Williams also lost his rifle, scrambling into a ditch. Middleton collected both weapons while posse members captured Williams. The posse "induced" their prisoner to tell what he knew about the McFadden party and to serve as their guide. Since cooperating with the posse insured his survival, Williams led them straight to the McFaddens.[8]

The McFaddens were headed to Montgomery, more than 100 miles to the south. Founded in Stephen F. Austin's colony in 1827, Montgomery was located twenty-five miles east of Washington-on-the-Brazos. The McFaddens knew someone who offered them refuge at a house located a mile south of Montgomery. The posse arrived shortly after the McFadden party, and Williams brought them to the house. The McFadden brothers barred and shuttered their hideout while posse members dismounted and surrounded the house. One-Eyed Williams obediently held the horses.

With the position secured, Middleton and at least one member of the posse rode into town "to get the necessary authority from the Justice of the Peace," although they were delayed because of the official's absence. While they waited, Bledsoe and another member of the McFadden party unsuspectingly rode up to the house. John Myrick and Frank Hooper ordered the startled Bledsoe to surrender, but he "sprang upon them both and came near wresting their guns from them...." In the scuffle Hooper's gun discharged, slightly wounding Bledsoe, but Myrick's rifle was broken. Bledsoe wrestled Hooper's gun away and began hitting him with it. Myrick seized another weapon and fired, inflicting another minor wound. By this time Jim Vaughan had reached the melee. Vaughan took aim, then fired a fatal bullet into Bledsoe.

Surrounded and with one confederate slain just outside their walls, the McFaddens lost heart. They were called upon to surrender, and after a conference agreed to negotiate. The Moderators agreed to surrender and pledged not to try to escape, "upon the understanding that they were to be taken safely to Shelby county and tried by the citizens, a majority to rule...." Although formal courts were in disarray, the McFaddens consented to submit to a "trial" by an assembly of citizens with a majority vote to decide their fate. If this irregular procedure represented "the best court then in Shelby County," as Watt Moorman and Eph Daggett contended, it was highly risky for a group of assassins.[9]

First the posse had to transport the McFadden brothers to Shelbyville, and it seemed they might not even get out of Montgomery. The McFaddens had friends in Montgomery – John Middleton thought that their leading ally was the county sheriff. After the posse and their prisoners mounted, they "found an entire captain's company assembled to protect these men...." But the posse members were heavily armed and resolute, and after maneuvering in silence they managed to "get entirely clear without molestation."[10]

Reaching Crockett, the posse learned that Tiger Jim Strickland had procured a writ for the arrest of Middleton, Moorman, and three other men who were not even members of the posse. The Houston County sheriff had received the writ, but Middleton persuaded the authorities that his posse was legal, then swore out a writ for the arrest of Strickland. A large crowd of armed men assembled, and one troublemaker "accosted" Middleton. When Watt Moorman distracted the man, another ruffian confronted the posse leader. Having worked up a thirst, these two men suddenly broke off the confrontation and marched into a nearby tavern. Middleton then mounted, formed up his men, "and by a concerted movement we wheeled our horses and placed the prisoners between us and the tavern where their friends were stationed, and went rapidly out of town."

A party estimated at sixty men pursued them, but Middleton pushed his posse nearly forty miles before stopping for a rest during the night. "We met with no more trouble," recorded Middleton. Approaching Shelby County, he sent five riders ahead to tell the citizenry to assemble in Shelbyville at noon on the coming Saturday, October 4, 1841.

When the party stopped at "widow Moore's" for breakfast, they were met by a large group of citizens. Placing the prisoners under the guard of the newcomers, the posse took a needed rest. When the new guards carelessly allowed John McFadden to escape. Middleton rode after him and recaptured his prisoner. Meanwhile, Buckskin Bill McFadden slipped out of his shackles and sprinted away, but "after a lively chase through the cane and timber," he was shot in the heel by Watt Moorman. Buckskin Bill, too, was recaptured, and Moorman's shot was measured at eighty-seven paces – impressive marksmanship against a running target.

As Middleton's party neared Shelbyville, they were met by almost 200 men who proudly escorted posse and prisoners into town. On Saturday at noon more than 300 citizens – probably the largest assembly in the short history of the sparsely-settled county – gathered on the courthouse square. All three McFadden brothers had admitted their guilt to the posse, "each confessing in the absence of others and ignorant of what had been said to them." After hearing their confessions, the crowd voted 174-0 to hang them, according to Middleton. Eph Daggett stated that "more than three hundred people" comprised the jury, while Dr. Ashcroft said that the verdict was decided "by a majority." Perhaps the women and children among a crowd of three hundred did not vote, resulting in the 174-0 tally. Whatever the count, the vote for execution was overwhelming. But onlooker Henry Runnells pled for mercy for fourteen-year-old Baily

Looking west toward Shelbyville, less than two miles away. Two McFadden brothers were executed at a hanging tree which stood near the pine tree in the center of the photo. *(Photo by the author)*

McFadden. After promising to reform, and "on account of his tender age," Baily "was pardoned" by the Shelbyville mob.[11]

Just over a mile northeast of town stood a grove of large oak trees. The mob transferred their prisoners from the courthouse to the oak grove, and began preparing to hang the two brothers from the same tree. Addressing the crowd, Bill and John McFadden expressed regret over the death of Lour, who was "killed by accident without any malicious intent whatever." But regarding Charles Jackson, the McFadden brothers "exulted in having been the means to rid mankind of so inhuman a monster." Recounting in detail Jackson's destruction of their homes, the McFaddens announced that "they felt justified in the sight of God and all unprejudiced men" in killing Jackson. "They had been bad men, they said, but were not afraid to die --"[12]

This account was recorded by Dr. Ashcroft. Eph Daggett also added details. "Bill McFadden cursed the Regulators, called them liars and told them that they would have to wade through blood." After venting his rage at his executioners, Buckskin Bill added a defiant prophecy: "And you fellows grinning now will bleed and die, damn you, to pay for this murder."[13]

A taunt came from the crowd. "Oh, damn you," snarled Bill, "you ain't worth killing." With his hands tied and a rope already noosed around his neck, Buckskin Bill impatiently tried to mount the horse being held for him beneath the tree limb. Because of the wound by his heel recently inflicted by Moorman, Bill had to be helped onto the horse. Moorman now "swung him up," and the crowd watched the McFaddens die.

Dr. Ashcroft called the double hanging "this tragedy." It was a classic example of a frontier lynching. Instead of the time and expense of jailing, trying, and executing two confessed assassins, the same result was achieved with prompt pursuit and a no-frills "trial," immediately followed by a hanging. Aside from the salary of Deputy Sheriff John Middleton, Shelby County incurred no expense – not even the cost of a gallows. Justice was swift, if extralegal, against the McFaddens. Since the days of Judge Charles Lynch, a significant portion of any frontier population would approve of such a pragmatic approach to justice. "The execution of the McFaddens produced no revulsion of public sentiment in their favor," commented Dr. Ashcroft. "They were looked upon as bad men, and as being no great loss to the country or society."[14]

With Charles Jackson dead, the Regulators needed a new leader. Watt Moorman had distinguished himself with the posse, and he had ridden with the Regulators who burned the Strickland and McFadden homes. "He could shoot straighter than any man I ever saw," stated Eph Daggett, whose sister, Helen, later married Moorman. "In stature he was about six feet, well proportioned, though spare, and of rare muscular power," described Dr. Ashcroft. "His hair was jet black and hung in profusion about his neck."[15]

At a large gathering of Regulators Moorman was elected commander, or colonel. "Colonel" Moorman led the Regulators

The Moorman home was a dogtrot log cabin with a long gallery across the front. Located on a hill nearby was the family cemetery. *(Courtesy Shelby County Historical Museum)*

for the next three years and he became the central character for the remainder of the Regulator-Moderator War.

In 1841 Charles Watt Moorman was in his mid-twenties. A native of Alabama, Watt remained in school until he was fifteen years of age. He had an infectious laugh but he was inclined toward "mischief" and was "the acknowledged leader of a set of scamps." His eyes were "black and piercing," and they restlessly shifted from one object to another. There was "a lurking devil in his eye, and an habitual and malicious contraction of the eyebrows." As a young man, Moorman "plunged into almost every variety of dissipation" and soon was in debt. "He forged a draft for two hundred and fifty dollars upon which he drew the money." When the fraud was discovered, Moorman fled to Texas, gravitating to Shelby County.[16]

The entire Moorman family – Watt's parents and six siblings – settled on land which today lies in southeastern Panola County. The Moormans built a cabin near Moorman Creek. Watt "would not work or confine himself to any kind of business," according to his brother-in-law, and for a time he lived with the Stricklands. He wrote amusing verse, and he enjoyed playing ten pins and billiards, although he was a bully who sometimes hit fellow players with a billiard cue. But Moorman did not depend on billiard cues for protection. In addition to his rifle, he belted a brace of pistols and a bowie knife around his waist. Moorman had *a large bois d'arc* walking stick" which he used to cane Moderators. Appropriate to his Regulator command, Colonel Moorman wore a military jacket, and he carried a hunting horn to summon his men with loud blasts.[17]

Colonel Moorman tracked down horse thief Squire Humphries, one of the assassins of Charles Jackson. Instead of fleeing Shelby County with other members of the assassination party, Humphries laid low, perhaps on his remote headright. Bad blood already existed between them, dating back to an incident before the Regulator-Moderator War, when Moorman still lived with the Stricklands. When Watt could not catch his horse one day, he angrily shot the animal, then borrowed a mount from Humphries. After more than a week, Humphries intercepted Moorman riding with a young lady. Despite Moorman's protests, Humphries retrieved his horse on the spot, putting Watt afoot and embarrassing him in front of the lady. On their next encounter, Moorman caned Humphries, delivering six licks before he could escape. Humphries became Moorman's enemy, and Watt did not consider their score settled.[18]

Colonel Moorman settled the score shortly after the execution of the McFaddens. Moorman and a party of Regulators tracked down Humphries and brought him to the vicinity of the hanging site. The captive bitterly announced that he "deserved death" for not leaving the county. "I was after you, too, Watt," continued Humphries. "You thrashed me with a hickory stick, then whipped me on the bare back, and now instead of my killing you you are going to hang me, so be at it. Let the thing be over and done with,"[19]

Lynching in Shelby County had escalated from flogging to hanging, following a farce of a trial, then to hanging with no pretense of a trial. But the substantial public support of the McFadden hangings, followed by the summary execution of Humphries, intimidated the Moderators. Although Regulators searched the countryside for more Moderators, Captain Merchant and his men suspended operations and went to ground.[20]

Robert Sanders, who settled in what became Shelby County in 1834, wrote a lengthy letter to his son in Tennessee on November 25, 1841. "I expect you have heard much said about the Regulators and Moderators in this county; they have been in actual rebellion." Sanders outlined the events to date, including the original murder committed by Jackson, the house burnings, and Jackson's assassination. "The Regulators then pursued every suspicious man, shot and hung, by order of a committee (as they termed it) of 7 men. The two partys have lost eleven or twelve this summer past; they bid defiance to the civil authority."[21]

Word spread about the murderous feuding in East Texas. In December 1841, Josiah Gregg passed through the vicinity of the feud on his way out of Texas after a six-month visit. The Regulator-Moderator conflict had been news since his arrival in Texas, and now he talked to citizens on the scene. "The people were in commotion – indeed we might say civil war during most of last summer and fall (in Shelby, Harrison and Panola counties)," explained Gregg to his journal. "There were two parties got up, calling themselves the *regulators* – the other the *moderators*. These formed themselves for a while into opposing armies – and during their difficulties several men were killed. But it seems their difficulties have been partly settled and all is quiet again."[22]

Gregg accurately described the Regulator-Moderator conflict after March, as well as the truce at year's end. Unfortunately, he also was correct in suggesting that "their difficulties have been *partly* settled…." The peace late in 1841 proved only temporary. Violence already had torn Harrison County, and erupted again in Shelby County in the spring of 1842.

Robert Potter, secretary of the navy during the Texas Revolution and senator during the Republic of Texas – the most prominent casualty of the Regulator-Moderator War. *(Courtesy Jefferson Historical Museum)*

# 5 War in Harrison County

*"If only I had a match to touch off this
cannon I would shoot your tongue
down your throat."*
—Harriet (Potter) Ames

The Regulator-Moderator malignancy began in Harrison County in 1840, several months before corresponding companies were organized in Shelby County. Two Moderators were killed late in 1840, and the Harrison County sheriff was slain by Regulators in January 1841 – three months before Charles Jackson murdered Joseph Goodbread. The spotlight of the Regulator-Moderator warfare soon shifted to Shelby County, which featured a greater number of killings and of participants. But violence in Harrison County produced victims of greater prominence than the killing fields of Shelby County. And when hostilities threatened to erupt into full-scale battle, Regulators and Moderators in Harrison County rode south to reinforce their Shelby County counterparts.

The most dangerous Regulator leader in Harrison County was William Pinckney Rose, a one-time soldier who did not hesitate to take direct action against the most prominent of adversaries. A native of North Carolina, Rose lived in Georgia, Louisiana and Mississippi, before restlessly moving in 1839 to the area which in that year became Harrison County. In his early fifties, he migrated to Texas with a large family that included married children. The newest Rose home was located on forested land a few miles west of Caddo Lake. A heavyset man who stood well over six feet, Rose was a tower of strength as patriarch of a frontier clan. Rose fought as a private at New Orleans under Andrew Jackson, but he claimed that he was a captain, and he was widely called "Captain Rose." Given to booming out profanities, he also was known as "Hell-roarin' Rose" and the "Lion of the Lakes." [1]

Captain Rose gathered a band of armed riders, many of them relatives or in-laws. These Regulators posed a threat in Harrison County, and the heavy-handed actions of Rose aroused lethal retaliation. "Two of the captain's most trusted men were killed in the service, Geo. W. Rembert and Isaac Hughes," wrote Rose's grandson, John H. McLean. Rembert, a son-in-law of Rose, and Hughes, brother of another son-in-law, were "both killed by Moderators," according to McLean. [2]

A posse of Regulators captured "two thieves..., who told of several of their clan that were in an out house, unarmed, and could easily be arrested." Rembert and two other Regulators went to capture these men, not suspecting that they were being lured "into a death trap." Somewhat carelessly the trio of Regulators rode up to the house and called out an order to surrender. The reply was a volley of gunfire from the house. Rembert was hit; he gamely returned fire, then dismounted from his horse, sat down at the base of a pine tree, and died. He was buried atop a rocky hill six miles northeast of Marshall.

Isaac Hughes was pulling corn in his field when he was approached by a large group of riders "under the command of a civil officer" who ordered Hughes to surrender "on some pretext." The near-sighted Hughes asked how many men were in the posse, and the answer was "about thirty." Hughes responded "that he could whip that number himself." The "civil officer" in charge -- apparently Sheriff John B. Campbell – chose to interpret this bravado as an excuse to achieve the posse's purpose. He gave the order to fire, and the volley killed Hughes instantly. Hughes was buried beside Rembert, and William P. Rose, "much grieved over the killing of these faithful lieutenants," made known his desire to be interred alongside Rembert and Hughes.

In an act of retribution typical of the Regulator-Moderator conflict, the brother of Isaac Hughes immediately sought vengeance.

In his deadly search for Sheriff John B. Campbell, Hughes evidently was assisted by Captain Rose. The first sheriff of Harrison County was George Mays, elected in 1839. Sheriff Mays, perhaps intimidated by the growing Regulator-Moderator violence, resigned in 1840, and soon was replaced by Dr. John B. Campbell. Dr. Campbell had taken up land in newly-organized Harrison County in December 1839. But in frontier Texas, physicians seldom collected cash for their services – payment usually consisted of eggs or ears of corn or some other produce – and Dr. Campbell saw opportunity as sheriff and tax collector.[3]

Sheriff Campbell was caught up in the Regulator-Moderator feud within months of his appointment. Perhaps, as sheriff, he was trying to moderate the Regulators of Captain Rose. But the execution of Isaac Hughes by a sheriff's posse brought revenge against Campbell. On Saturday, January 23, 1841, Sheriff Campbell was "assassinated" in Port Caddo, gunned down by the brother of Hughes and, perhaps, by Captain Rose.[4]

With a sheriff brazenly slain on a public street, Regulator-Moderator anarchy reigned in Harrison County. Within three weeks of Campbell's death, the office of sheriff and tax collector was filled by L.H. Dillard. But less than four months later, on July 12, Sheriff Dillard left his increasingly dangerous post. About six weeks later, around the first of September, Daniel Minor and D. Morriss were killed by Captain Rose and his Regulators.[5]

A persistent story concerned a newcomer to Harrison County. Encountering a band of armed riders, he was asked if he were a Regulator or a Moderator. Unaware of the conflict and pressed for an answer, he replied in favor of Regulators. It proved to be the wrong answer, and he was badly beaten. Presently the newcomer encountered another group of rough-looking men, who posed the same question. Hoping to avoid another beating, the newcomer hastily identified himself as a Regulator. Once again he guessed wrong, and absorbed another pummeling. This tale probably is apocryphal, but was so tenaciously repeated that it likely contained a kernel of truth regarding the atmosphere of lawlessness prevailing in Harrison County.[6]

One man in a possession of authority, unafraid of strife,

decided to take action to restore order. Senator Robert Potter, a contentious individual, triggered the most dramatic and memorable incidents of the Regulator-Moderator War.

Like Sam Houston and William Barret Travis, Potter arrived in Texas with scandal in his background. A native of North Carolina, fifteen-year-old Potter joined the U.S. Navy as a midshipman in 1815. Before adventure-seeking American youngsters began running away from home to become western cowboys, they went to sea, but Bob Potter was not interested in life aboard some whaler. The War of 1812 had just ended, and young Potter responded to a patriotic urge to serve his country. Throughout his life he gravitated to public service, as well as adventure and danger. But with the war ended, there was not much adventure or danger in the Navy. Midshipman Potter served aboard several ships which sometimes chased smugglers and slavers. But promotion was slow in the peacetime Navy, and in 1821 Midshipman Potter resigned and returned to North Carolina to study law. During the next decade and a half Potter became embroiled in brawls, duels, adultery, and savage maimings.[7]

Potter was a magnet for trouble. He was a volatile man, passionate and restless and hot-tempered. Some malevolent aspect of his character triggered a self-destructive need for enemies, and his abrasive conduct assured him a steady supply of adversaries. A masterful orator, Potter repeatedly showered ridicule and vitriol on acquaintances and public figures, and he rarely hesitated to go into action against perceived enemies. Handsome and capable of great charm, Potter was a ladies' man. He compulsively pursued desirable females, regardless of marital status – theirs or his.

The young lawyer ran for election to the North Carolina House of Commons in 1824, but he was defeated by incumbent Jesse Bynum. With virulent spite, Potter challenged Bynum to a duel. When Bynum refused to fight, Potter challenged his second, who also declined. Later Potter instigated a free-for-all at a party. During the melee Bynum's hand was cracked and Potter was speared by the slender blade of a sword cane. Both men were arrested.

Perhaps Potter's physical courage impressed the male electorate. Potter was elected to the House of Commons in 1826 and to the U.S. Congress two years later. In 1828 he married Isabelle

Taylor, who bore him a son and a daughter. But in Washington, Potter allegedly "became infatuated with a beautiful heiress,"[8] and needed to rid himself of his wife so that he could remarry. Back in North Carolina, he assaulted and castrated a middle-aged Methodist minister and accused him of adultery with Mrs. Potter. Then he attacked and castrated a seventeen-year-old distant relative of his wife, again charging adultery. As news of this brutal scandal spread, North Carolinians coined a new term for assault-castration: "potterizing."

No lawyer was willing to defend Potter, so he prepared his own case. Potter's defense was built around "unwritten law," but under written law he was convicted, fined $1,000, and sentenced to six months in jail. His wife divorced Potter and legally changed the last name of their children. Somehow the irrepressible Potter persuaded the voters to re-elect him to the legislature in 1834. Then, at Christmas 1834, Potter and a fellow member of the House named Cotten were involved in a disreputable scene over a card game. Apparently Potter, a heavy loser, tried to make off with the pot but Cotten fought him until Potter pulled a pistol. Early in 1835 the legislature voted to expel Potter, who then decided to start over in Texas.

Potter arrived in Nacogdoches in July 1835, when problems between Mexico and its northern province of Texas had risen to explosive levels. Outspoken by nature and confident in a leadership role from his years in Congress and the North Carolina House of Commons, Potter asserted himself during public meetings at Nacogdoches. An advocate for Texas independence from Mexico, Potter enlisted in Captain Thomas J. Rusk's company of Nacogdoches Independent Volunteers in October 1835. Less than two months later Potter resigned from the army to petition the new Provisional Government for a commission in a proposed Texas navy. The six-year veteran of the U.S. Navy received a commission, and he also won election as a delegate to a General Convention which met at Washington-on-the-Brazos.

Potter and Sam Houston were the two delegates who were the most experienced in government affairs. From the first day, Potter offered motions and resolutions, and served on key committees. He was one of fifty-nine men who signed the Texas Declaration of Independence, and when an *ad interim* government was organized, Potter was appointed secretary of the navy. With General Santa Anna and his Mexican Army marching eastward from San Antonio, General Sam Houston was sent into the field to organize resistance. The convention at Washington-on-the-Brazos adjourned, and Secretary Potter rode toward the coast to inspect Texas ports and ships.

The Provisional Government provided for the purchase of four armed schooners late in 1835, and these warships soon clashed with vessels of the Mexican Navy. One Mexican ship was captured and added to the Texas Navy. A steamboat was utilized to help defend Galveston, making six vessels in Secretary Potter's little fleet.

At the port of Velasco it was decided to ship residents to Galveston, where a concentrated defense would be organized. But as Secretary Potter and a small party rode toward Galveston, they encountered refugees, Texas settlers fleeing ahead of the Mexican army – participants in the "Runaway Scrape." Although Potter directed most civilians to the two ships waiting at Velasco, he took personal charge of an attractive young woman.

She was twenty-six-year-old Harriet Moore Page, whose father, Dr. Francis Moore, Jr., was editor of *The Telegraph and Texas Register,* and whose husband was marching with General Houston's rag-tag army. Solomon Page had gambled his family into poverty, and he had moved from New Orleans to Texas for a new start. Harriet was swept into the Runaway Scrape. She placed her little boy on someone's wagon and trudged along muddy roads carrying her infant daughter. With the gallantry he typically displayed toward desirable females, Potter offered to transport Harriet and her children into Velasco. A slave took the children onto his mount, while Harriet was placed behind Potter. "Never was a woman treated in a more kind and thoughtful manner, than I was by Colonel Potter," reminisced Harriet. "Himself a perfect gentleman, he treated me with all the deference due a queen....."[9]

Potter installed Harriet and her children aboard his flagship, the armed schooner *Flash.* Accommodations in Galveston were strained by refugees, so Harriet remained in her quarters aboard the

*Flash* for weeks. Sadly, her daughter died and was buried on Galveston Island. In the meantime, the Texas navy continued to block Mexican ships from landing supplies and reinforcements. Potter loudly complained about General Houston's leadership during the Runaway Scrape, and his criticism continued even after the spectacular Texan victory at San Jacinto. When the wounded Houston decided to seek medical treatment in New Orleans, he was refused passage on a naval vessel by President David G. Burnet and Secretary Potter. Potter soon set out for New Orleans, supposedly on department business, sailing aboard the *Pocket,* a brig which had been commandeered by the Texas navy.

Sam Houston did not soon forget his resentment of Potter's public criticism and behavior. Years later Houston stated that Potter's "infamy was wider than the world and deeper than perdition…."[10]

Potter resigned from the navy and traveled to New Orleans with a small party which included Harriet Page and her son, Joe. Harriet and Joe departed New Orleans with Potter by steamboat, journeying up the Mississippi River, then northwest up the Red River to Shreveport. Potter, Harriet, and Joe moved to a cabin on the Sabine River in Shelby County, then in 1837 established their home on Caddo Lake. Potter persuaded Harriet that since she had not married Page in a Catholic ceremony her marriage was invalid in Texas since it had not been performed by a priest. She went along with that rationalization, and agreed to an informal frontier wedding on September 5, 1836, in Shelby County before four witnesses. She testified that, "according to the custom of the country, the little assembly gathered to see us wedded; the ceremony was a very simple one in these days in that country, but it was just as binding as if judge and clergy were present."[11] Apparently Robert and Harriet did not jump the broom – another pioneer marriage custom – and "our piney woods wedding" later proved not binding in a court of law. Harriet also related that Potter wrote a legal statement of their marriage, but this document – if it ever existed – could not be produced when she later needed it in court. "He always told me he was an old bachelor," she insisted.[12] But when Potter learned that his ex-wife had died, he told Harriet about his first marriage and his extra-marital affair while serving in Congress. In 1840, after Harriet had resided with Potter for four years, the forsaken Solomon Page obtained a divorce.

Potter procured a lakeside headright from the Republic of Texas. Claiming that he was the head of a family – and thus entitled to more acreage – Potter received a league and a *labor* of land, a total of 4,605 acres, located in a lovely but sparsely settled wilderness overlooking Lake Caddo. He built a log cabin and outbuildings on a promontory that became known as "Potter's Point."

"A place more beautiful than Potter's Point it would be impossible to imagine," wrote Harriet in her eighties. She described her home with poetic grace. "I never tired of admiring the scenery that lay about my new home. Our house stood upon a jutting promontory that rose into a hill set in the midst of one of the grandest timber belts in Texas." A steep bank led downward 200 feet to "the

Painting by archaeologist Claude McCrocklin of the log cabin and outbuildings of Robert Potter's home. Potter waves to Harriet, standing on the plank gallery of their house. McCrocklin based this scene on his archaeological work at Potter's Point and on the detailed account of Harriet Ames. *(Courtesy Claude W. McCrocklin of Shreveport)*

most romantically beautiful lake that I've ever beheld. For eight miles one could look across to the opposite shore over a great sheet of sparkling water that washed up into the white beach below the cliff...."[13]

"Islands covered with tall trees rose out of the lake," she continued, "and these dropped from their shores garlands and loops of wild flowers and graceful vines, like dainty fingers diving into the water to clasp their own beautiful reflection...." Harriet loved to watch morning mists rise above the water, and the "crimson and purple glory" of sunsets across the lake. She constantly responded to the floral beauty around her. "I often wonder if ever so many flowers grew in any other woods. The ground was covered with them in gray, luxuriant masses that made the forest bright with color, and among the grand trees of the old forests flourished all manner

Painting of Harriet and her son Joe looking west across Caddo Lake from Potter's Point. The path in front of them leads to the bluff and to steps cut down to the lakeside. Harriet is dressed as she describes in her memoirs. *(Courtesy Claude W. McCrocklin of Shreveport)*

of wild fruits, grapes, plums and persimmons, with the red haws, and sweet berries. Nature had spared no pain to make complete the beauty of this spot...." This statement could have been made about most of the Regulator-Moderator countryside.

With the help of hired hands and slaves, Potter cleared and cultivated fields and constructed fences and outbuildings. Steps were cut into the bluff leading to the lake. The main cabin, built of logs, had a sleeping loft and a detached kitchen.[14] There was a gallery -- later called a porch -- across the front, and a puncheon floor inside. Potter and Harriet brought a son and a daughter into the world in this isolated frontier home. Harriet's brother, George Moore, also lived and worked at Potter's Point, and her firstborn son, Joe Page, was part of the household.

Potter often left on business trips to Shreveport or to Clarksville, located in north Texas. In 1840 he was elected to the Texas Senate, which meant long trips to Austin. Senator Potter, as usual, became an active member of the legislative body. He was also active socially. Just before starting the long ride home from Austin following the congressional session of 1841-1842, Potter wrote a will, dated February 11, 1842. He made sizeable bequests to three members of his love life: Mrs. Sophie Ann Mayfield of Austin; Mrs. Mary W. Chalmers of Clarksville; and "Mrs. Harriet A. Page." Potter left more land to Mrs. Mayfield and Mrs. Chalmers than he did to Harriet, and the bequest to Mrs. Mayfield included the Potter home place. Understandably Potter said nothing to Harriet about the will.[15]

Potter arrived home in late February 1842. He brought with him from Austin a proclamation offering a $500 reward for the capture of William P. Rose. The proclamation, dated November 15, 1841, and signed by President Mirabeau B. Lamar, accused Rose of murdering Sheriff John B. Campbell of Harrison County in January 1841, and Daniel Minor and D. Morriss on or about September 1, 1841.[16] Other Regulators may have been involved in these three killings, but Potter targeted Rose as the leader and chief troublemaker. Aside from the tactical advantage of arresting the most formidable Regulator, Potter – as usual – had a personal score to settle.

There were rumors that Potter, the incurable womanizer,

had once made advances toward a female member of the Rose family, and that Rose had opposed his candidacy to the Texas Senate. For these and other reasons, a bitter enmity developed between Potter and Rose. Harriet referred to him as "Old Rose," and said that he "made himself a terror to his acquaintances. He was feared and disliked by all," she emphasized.[17]

"The sheriff was killed by 'Old Rose'," added Harriet. Potter's intention was to "moderate" Rose and his Regulators, and he was regarded as a leader for the Moderators in the area. "Col. Potter belonged to the 'Moderator's' party and Old Rose was to be imprisoned and tried by law...," stated Harriet.[18] Potter raised a large posse, although the seventeen men who rode with him to arrest Rose, like most possemen of the nineteenth century, were motivated primarily by their projected share of the posted reward. Even if identification with the Moderator faction was only a secondary motivation, by riding in force against a prominent – and dangerous – Regulator leader, the Potter posse exacerbated the Regulator-Moderator conflict in Harrison County.

Robert Potter led his seventeen-man posse to Rose's wilderness home, located between Marshall and Lake Caddo, on Tuesday morning, March 1, 1842. Rose was supervising slaves working to clear a plot of land. As his slaves began burning piles of brush, Rose saw Potter and his posse riding toward the Rose home. Realizing that he was hopelessly outnumbered, Rose had a slave pile brush on top of him. Potter questioned Rose's eighteen-year-old son, Preston, and after failing to learn the location of his prey, he rode into the clearing to talk to the slaves. Again he learned nothing, and with no sign of Rose, Potter led his men back down the trail.

As the posse disappeared, Rose emerged from hiding and sent Preston to follow the posse to a fork in the road. Preston returned to report that the posse had split, with nine men continuing with Potter. George Moore, Harriet's brother, and a few others rode all the way to Potter's Point. Potter told Harriet that he thought Rose would surrender with no trouble, but she was worried. "When Old Rose hears that you have been hunting for him he will come here tonight and try to kill you."[19]

Harriet tried to persuade him to have the men at Potter's

Point sleep inside the main cabin, but he refused and prepared to go to bed. The cabin contained a number of firearms, including a "small cannon loaded with buckshot." This weapon must have been a ship's swivel gun, a light cannon which did not require a gun carriage and that was easy to transport and to mount. Potter was tired from his day in the saddle, but while he slept, Harriet remained restless. When she heard dogs barking she tried to rouse Potter, but he remained asleep. Harriet's fears were well founded.

Rose had no intention of waiting for another posse. Determined to seize the offensive, he quickly raised his own posse. His son Preston, son-in-law John W. Scott, and several other relatives and friends rode with him. This armed band pushed hard for Potter's Point, arriving during the middle of the night. Rose and his men crept into position, but not carefully enough to prevent Potter's dogs from barking. It was early on Wednesday morning, March 2, 1842, six years to the day – also on a Wednesday – that Potter had signed the Texas Declaration of Independence.

Harriet was up before dawn. She roused a slave boy to go out and grind corn meal for breakfast, and he was seized by the Regulators. When the boy failed to return Harriet sent her brother George to look for him. George, too, was quietly overpowered. An old man named Hezekiah ventured out to feed the hogs, his first chore of the day. With the skies beginning to lighten, Harriet decided to look for the boy and her brother. As she stepped outside toward the detached kitchen, several men rose from concealment. Hezekiah took a shotgun blast to his buttocks, but Harriet eluded a couple of men and darted back to the cabin. Other shots were fired, and Potter leaped from his bed.

"I suppose all the men are killed," blurted Harriet, "they have just killed one." She wanted to fort up and defend the cabin. "We can defend ourselves," she insisted. "I will stand by you as long as we both live."

Potter peered through a crack between the logs along the back wall. Spotting several assailants, he decided to try to escape out the front door to the lake, "as he was a fine swimmer," he reminded Harriet. Perhaps, too, it may have crossed his mind that the defense of the cabin would seriously endanger the children inside.

Slipping outside with a rifle in his hands, Potter bolted across the yard, vaulted over the fence, then scrambled down the steps leading to the beach. Shots were fired after him, and the attackers ran to the bluff and continued to shoot, without effect. Although his rifle was empty, John W. Scott aggressively followed Potter down the steep bank.

Painting of the Caddo Lake site where Robert Potter was killed. He was shot approximately where the boat appears in the left foreground. Left of center is the stepped path leading up to the cabin at the top of the bluff. *(Courtesy Claude W. McCrocklin of Shreveport)*

At the bottom of the cut steps were three big cypress trees. Under fire from the bluff, Potter leaned his rifle against one of the trees, waded into the lake, and dove underwater. Scott seized Potter's loaded rifle and went to the water's edge. Potter swam underwater until he needed air, and when his head bobbed up, Scott was waiting with the rifle at his shoulder. He shot Potter in the back of the head. He sank beneath the waters without a struggle. (Scott kept Potter's rifle. He had married the widowed daughter of William P. Rose, Ann Rose McLean, who had two little boys by her first marriage. Her younger son, John McLean, who became a prominent Methodist minister, recalled that during his boyhood he "hunted squirrels with the gun that did the execution."[20]]

Back on the promontory, Harriet anxiously emerged from the cabin, but "Old Rose leveled his gun at me and ordered me to go into the house." Harriet refused to go inside, even though Rose continued to brandish his rifle at her. Then Scott reappeared in the yard from below. "What are you abusing Mrs. Potter for?" Scott snapped at Rose. "She has never done you any harm; come on let's go. We have done what we came to do."

"Now what do you think of your pretty Bobby?" sneered Rose. Harriet looked longingly at her little artillery piece loaded with buckshot. "If only I had a match to touch off this cannon I would shoot your tongue down your throat."

Insisting that Harriet "was too brave a woman to kill," Scott pulled Rose away from the cabin. Other Regulators released the boy and Harriet's brother, then the entire posse left Potter's Point.

Harriet and her brother found the fallen Hezekiah still alive. They dressed his wounds, then descended to the lake to search for Potter. Harriet thought that he might have escaped to one of the numerous small islands. She and her brother spent the day rowing from island to island, "until I despaired of ever finding him alive...." During the night a violent thunderstorm swept across the lake. The next morning the little cannon was brought down to the shoreline. There was an old superstition that a cannon shot would bring a drowned body to the surface. But before a shot could be fired, Potter's corpse was sighted, floating close to the shore.

The body was carried to the cabin to be prepared for burial.

"In his trousers pocket was the match I had needed so sorely to fire the cannon upon his murderers," lamented Harriet.[21] A couple of friends, who must have heard rumors of the incident at Potter's Point the previous day, came to offer assistance. Potter had told Harriet that he would like to be buried on "a beautiful knoll on the hill in front of the house where a clump of tall trees grew." A grave was dug there, and Potter was interred without the shelter of a coffin. A few cypress planks were laid over him before the grave was filled. In 1928 it was decided to relocate Potter's body in the state cemetery in Austin, but when the grave was opened, only a few bone fragments remained to be transferred.[22]

Harriet left her children in the care of a servant named Hannah, and, accompanied by her brother and another man, traveled to Clarksville to file charges before District Judge John T. Mills. Identifying herself as "Harriet A. Potter," on March 25, 1842, she charged ten men with the murder of her "husband" -- William P. Rose, Preston Rose, John W. Scott, Stephen Peters, Samuel Perkins, Isaac Jones, William Smith, Calvin Miller, Sandy Miller, and James Williams. On April 6, the grand jury of Red River County returned a true bill against all but Williams and the two Millers. Bail was refused, but since there was no jail in Clarksville, Sheriff Edward West took the seven prisoners to the nearest lockup, in Nacogdoches, more than 170 miles to the south. The sheriff of Nacogdoches County, keenly aware of the murderous Regulator-Moderator conflict then raging in adjacent Shelby County, refused to accept such controversial prisoners in his jail. Sheriff West rode east to Shelbyville, where he obtained an order of incarceration from District Judge William B. Ochiltree.[23]

When Harriet returned from Clarksville to Potter's Point, she was staggered to learn that her three-year-old daughter had been scalded to death while Hannah was making soap. It may have been some consolation that the Texas Senate passed a Resolution honoring Senator Potter: "...RESOLVED, that we deeply deplore the loss of the talented Senator. RESOLVED, that in further testimony of respect, the Senators wear crepe on the left arm for thirty days...." The entire resolution was published in *The Telegraph and Texas Register* on July 20, 1842. Further consolation came just over a month later when Harriet married Charles Ames. Employed by Potter to help with his farm, Ames proved to be a hard-working husband and father. Less than six months into their marriage, in January 1843, Potter's will was probated in Clarksville. Harriet was unaware of the existence of the will, written just three weeks before Potter's death, and certainly she was unaware that two other women had shared Potter's affections – and his bequests. Learning that Mrs. Sophie Mayfield of Austin was awarded the Potter home place by the will, Harriet and Charles Ames began a legal campaign to reclaim what now was their family home.[24]

Robert Potter's killers assembled a crack legal team led by General Thomas J. Rusk and future Texas Governor J. Pinckney Henderson. Rusk and Henderson were trained attorneys from South Carolina and North Carolina respectively, and Rusk had served two years as chief justice of Texas. Rusk and Henderson formed a partnership in February 1841 which became the most noted legal firm in the Republic of Texas. These able defense lawyers arranged for bail in May 1842, and obtained a change of venue to Nacogdoches County. The case went to trial in district court in the spring of 1843, and Harriet Ames journeyed to Nacogdoches to testify. But Rusk and Henderson won dismissal of the case for lack of evidence.[25]

Regulators could only have been emboldened by another triumph over the legal system. With murderous impunity, a posse of Regulators had slain a highly prominent leader of Moderators, Senator Robert Potter, who bore a proclamation endorsed by the president of the Republic. They suffered no legal consequences except for a relatively brief incarceration while awaiting trial. With the courts of Texas posing no deterrence for Regulators or Moderators, old scores could be taken up with little fear of sheriffs or judges or juries.

The growing body count soon included the founder of Marshall, Peter Whetstone. In 1841, two years after Harrison County was created, Whetstone donated acreage for a townsite from his headright as a married resident when the Texas Declaration of Independence was signed. Although semi-literate, Whetstone set aside extra acreage for a university and a Masonic temple that would house a girls' school on the ground floor.[26] Despite his benevolence, rumors persisted that Whetstone had a violent past, and during the Regulator-Moderator conflict he "took sides with the Moderators," according to Eph Daggett, "and sent his boys down into Shelby County to fight the Regulators." Whetstone had two sons, Anderson and Warrick, who were old enough to take up arms during the Regulator-Moderator War. Daggett explained that the Whetstones had relatives in Shelby County, adding that Potter and his sons were "good fighters." Furthermore, the Whetstones "opposed old man Rose and his party."[27]

Peter Whetstone incurred the enmity of "Colonel" William T. Boulware, a diehard Regulator who had built a blockhouse on his property to defend against possible attack. On Monday, November 13, 1843, Whetstone found himself hunted by Regulators in the town he had founded. He was flushed from a thicket just south of Marshall (where the railroad depot later would be built). Covered with a rifle, Whetstone said to the Regulator, "You have known me and I have never harmed you, why should you take my life?"[28]

"All right," shrugged the Regulator. "Get by, but don't let anyone know you passed me."

Soon afterward, Whetstone ventured downtown, entering a store on the east side of the square, later the site of the Capitol Hotel. There Whetstone encountered Boulware. Both men were drinking, and they quarreled. When Whetstone left, Boulware followed him outside and shot him dead. Whetstone was buried near his home west of Marshall, while his killer was never indicted. Noted citizens and officials of the Republic and county were slain but the fledgling legal machinery of Harrison County simply ceased to operate against Regulator-Moderator feudists.

The assassination of Sheriff Campbell in 1841, the killing of Senator Potter in 1842, and the murder of Peter Whetstone in 1843 in the town he founded, each took place less than twenty miles from the home of Judge John Hansford, who "had married a respected widow."[29] Hansford's homestead was located near Jonesville in eastern Harrison County. After Judge Hansford retreated there in 1841 from the Pulaski courtroom he had regarded as unsafe, he was forced to resign as district judge and devoted his time to developing his property. Having witnessed firsthand the threatening presence of Regulators, and keenly aware of the nearby Regulator murders of prominent men, Hansford must have been relieved that he had distanced himself from the Regulator-Moderator conflict.

In 1843 Hansford, frustrated in his efforts to collect a debt, obtained a writ of sequestration -- "the legal seizure of property for security"-- which enabled him to take possession of some slaves.

The Scott family moved the remains of William Pinckney Rose to the Scottsville Cemetery. The Rose monument is the tallest in the cemetery, and the statement reads: "HE WAS A TOWER OF STRENGTH IN WAR, IN STATE, AT HOME." *(Photo by the author)*

The owner of the slaves was a Regulator or had Regulator connections, so a Regulator posse assembled to confront Hansford over the matter. One Sunday morning in January 1844, Hansford and his wife returned home from church services to find a band of Regulators waiting for them. The armed men demanded that Hansford turn over the slaves. Deserted by his usual sense of prudence, Hansford refused and was shot dead. Hansford joined Robert Potter as the second member of the Texas Congress slain by Regulators. Decades later, also like Potter, Hansford had a county in the Panhandle named in his honor.[30]

It is not known if William Pinckney Rose was involved in the Hansford killing, or if he was one of the Regulator reinforcements who rode into Shelby County in 1844. Rose survived the Regulator-Moderator War, only to contract pneumonia a few years later, dying at sixty-two on January 23, 1850. A friend of Harriet Ames traveled to Potter's Point with the news. "He told me that his death was a terrible one," recalled Harriet with apparent relish. "A violent thunderstorm was raging and on his death bed Old Rose lay cursing God."[31] As Rose had requested, he was buried beside George Rembert and Isaac Hughes. More than half a century later, Rose's relatives transferred his remains to the handsome cemetery in Scottsville. Regardless of the understandable feelings of Harriet Ames toward "Old Rose," his family remembered him as a heroic soldier and frontier patriarch. Accordingly, the tallest memorial in the cemetery was erected in his memory, and the following statement was engraved on the stone:

> A soldier in the War of 1812,
> A Hero at the Battle of New Orleans.
> He was a Tower of Strength in War,
> in State, at Home.

Harriet and Charles Ames lived out their marriage at Potter's Point. Although the legal status of their home had not been settled, they added split-rail fencing and erected slave cabins and various outbuildings. They raised a large family there before Ames died in 1866 in the twenty-fourth year of his marriage to Harriet. Sophie Mayfield died in 1852, having never pressed her claim to the Potter bequest in faraway northeast Texas. But later her heirs filed suit for the property, and the case went to the Texas Supreme Court in 1875. Chief Justice Oran M. Roberts handed down the decision that there had never been a legal marriage between Potter and Harriet, and

Monument erected at Potter's Point to honor Harriet Ames, "Bravest Woman in Texas." Harriet's log home stood a short distance to the right, and just behind the monument is a steep bluff 200 feet above Caddo Lake. *(Photo by the author)*

therefore Potter's will was valid. After nearly four decades at Potter's Point, Harriet, now in her mid-sixties, had to leave her home and live with grown children in New Orleans until her death in 1902.[32]

Harriet, who had endured hardships and tragedies as a pioneer mother and companion at Potter's Point, who courageously defied Potter's killers and caused their arrest and trial, was regarded by many as "the bravest woman in Texas," although there were other worthy candidates for this designation. Harriet proudly recalled an incident that occurred at Potter's Point: "I...was so widely known as 'the bravest woman in Texas' that one day a man arrived at our place who had ridden sixty miles to see me."[33] She became a sympathetic character of great appeal, and perhaps it is ungallant to suggest that some measure of that appeal might be misplaced.

By the time Harriet reflected on her life while composing her memoirs, she had convinced herself that from the time Robert Potter first encountered her, he "was weaving a net around me that it was impossible to break."[34] Harriet's memoirs, like any personal reminiscence, were told from the vantage point of the author. Subconsciously – perhaps consciously – the elderly lady portrayed herself as favorably as possible to her loved ones and to anyone else who might read her recollections. Robert Potter, of course, had manipulated Harriet for his own purposes so certainly she was entitled to record her version of events. But it strains credulity that she naively swallowed one deception after another from Potter with no suspicions, no doubts. She was attracted to Potter because he was handsome and charming – and because he could provide protection and a home for her and her children. Harriet accepted Potter for her own pragmatic – as well as romantic – reasons, but when she ventured with him to the Texas frontier she proved hardy and courageous. Certainly she suffered heartbreak and tragedy on the frontier, and the loss of the home she helped carve from the wilderness was lamentable. Harriet was not a paragon of marital virtue – at least not until her third coupling, with Charles Ames – but perhaps she earned whatever measure of respect and sympathy that later generations would choose to bestow.

The rugged features of Judge Ochiltree suggest the formidable personality displayed to the people of Shelbyville. *(Courtesy Shelby County Historical Museum)*

# 6 Regulator Ascendancy

*"Moorman's company now had largely the
ascendancy in the county, and... controlled
public affairs in their own way."*
—Dr. Levi Ashcroft

While Regulator-Moderator violence in Harrison County
felled ranking public officials, fighting continued sporadically in
Shelby County, and hatreds steadily intensified. The atmosphere
was so menacing that in December 1841, nearly a score of respectable
citizens sent a petition to the Texas Congress requesting protection:

To the Members of the Congress of the Republic of Texas

We, the subscribers, Citizens of the Counties of Shelby and
San Augustine, most respectfully represent to your Hon.
body; that, feeling a deep interest in the prosperity of Texas
generally, a wish to see the Laws of the Republic fully and
faithfully administered for the protection of the life and
property of her Citizens, and to secure every man in his
rights guaranteed by the Constitution, and to avert what
we now fear a Civil War, would ask the indulgence of
Congress and the protection of the same.

We do not wish nor shall attempt to detail to your Honorable
body the hundreds of violations of the law which have been,
and are now being inflicted upon the Citizens of these

Counties, nor do we ask for aide to avenge any particular personal wrong; but approach you, having the good of the County at heart, and feeling conscious, that you will afford that protection so much desired.

Armed bands of self styled Regulators, assuming to themselves the right and power to distribute Justice to whom it belongs, have assembled and are now in daily action, governed and influenced by the worst feelings of man's nature, losing sight of all that is human and just – pursuing their victims to the Grave, proscribing others, -- laying the finest farms in the country waste, driving from their homes and useful pursuits, honest citizens; spreading terror abroad in the land and sapping the foundation of all that is peaceful and social; holding themselves in readiness to serve the citizens or strangers for hire; subject to be influenced by prejudice or partiality; having no fixed principal tending to the good of the community in any way – and no Law but Force.

Under such a state of things we now live, and fearing without the speedy interference of Congress the evil will increase, We humbly ask of your Honorable Body this protection, that we have a right to expect.

Respectfully

| | |
|---|---|
| N.B. Garner | Lyne Buckley |
| James H. Lucas | W.H. Dunn |
| Charles Wood | R.C. McDaniel |
| E. Rains | A.C. Baker |
| E.O. Legrand | Wade Horton |
| Thos. S. Wiggins | H.W. Sublett |
| J.D. Rains | W.B. Thompson |
| F.W. Daniels | John S. Ford |
| J.S. Collins | R.P. Hart[1] |

Typical of the standing of these men was John S. Ford, twenty-six years of age and a public-spirited physician and lawyer in San Augustine. In later years Ford distinguished himself during the Mexican War, fought Comanches as a Texas Ranger captain, and led Confederates to victory at Palmito Ranch, the last battle of the Civil War. But the pleas of such men as Ford brought no response from Congress or from Sam Houston, recently inaugurated for his second term as president. Although President Houston had lived and practiced law in both Nacogdoches and San Augustine, he was preoccupied by severe troubles with Mexico and other pressing difficulties and so he ignored the Regulator-Moderator turbulence for the time being.

With no curb on his actions, Watt Moorman consolidated his power in Shelby County. Colonel Moorman enrolled about 100 men in his Regulator company, while "more than half of the citizens of the county" identified with the Regulators: "A large number of worthless scamps, who had nothing to lose, and who were willing to do almost any act of villainy, or blood, so they were protected," observed a disapproving Dr. Ashcroft. "Strange as it may appear, these vampires were sustained by the better portion of the company, so blinded were they by prejudice and passion. No matter with what crime a man was charged, if he belonged to the company, he was protected." Even though the Moderator company was dormant, word spread that anyone who "refused to join the Regulators were classed by them as Moderators."[2]

Moorman controlled Shelbyville through the intimidating presence of armed Regulators. "If a Moderator, that is any one who did not belong to the Regulators, had business at the county seat, he found it hazardous in the extreme to venture there to attend to it." There were insults and chilling threats. "Numbers of unoffending young men were horsewhipped or otherwise sorely abused for no other reason that they had ventured to visit town without permission."

A rural schoolteacher named Burrows became outspoken against Moorman's dictatorial methods. Moorman soon learned of the young teacher's critical remarks, and when Burrows next visited Shelbyville, he was intercepted by Watt, "who, as usual was surrounded by a number of his men, armed to the teeth." No one dared interfere as Moorman, with his bois d'arc walking stick in one hand and a bowie knife in the other, brutally whipped Burrows.

Burrows could not "forget or forgive an insult of that character," but he realized that if he tried to "engage in honorable combat" he would be slain by Moorman's bodyguards. Burrows "determined to obtain satisfaction in another manner more in keeping with the conduct of his enemy," and two of his friends were daring enough to help. Burrows and his well-armed comrades set an ambush "on a road he knew the Colonel was compelled to pass alone...." Moorman was widely known as a "libertine," and it might be speculated that he was traveling without his usual bodyguard to rendezvous with a sweetheart, perhaps a married one. For whatever reason, Moorman rode alone toward the ambush site, as expected. Burrows, armed with a double-barreled shotgun, fired first, but he succeeded mostly in blasting a nearby oak tree. One ball missed the tree and struck Moorman in the fleshy part of his leg. Spurring his horse, Moorman galloped away, while the shots of the other two men whistled past harmlessly.

Moorman thundered into Shelbyville "roaring and frothing like a mad bull, cursing all Moderators...as a set of cowards and scoundrels who were afraid to meet a man in open fight, but who laid in ambush to shoot men in the back." It occurred to some listeners that Moorman "had done the same thing on more than one occasion." Burrows and his friends apparently left the country, perhaps crossing the Sabine River, because they were not apprehended by the Regulators.

Not as fortunate or elusive was a Moderator assassin named Boatright, one of the gunmen who had killed Charles Jackson and his companion. Boatright scrambled across the Sabine River to Louisiana, losing his shoes, coat, and hat in his desperate escape. He found employment on a plantation in DeSoto Parish. When word of Boatright's location reached Shelby County, half a dozen Regulators were dispatched to "arrest" him. The Regulator posse found Boatright picking cotton and took him into extralegal custody. Returning to Texas, the posse was met near Watson's Ferry by Colonel Moorman and a large party of Regulators.[3]

One of Moorman's men was Charles L. Mann, a member of the Shelby County bar. Dr. Ashcroft, who also practiced law on occasion, grumbled about Mann that the legal profession was "never disgraced by a more dastardly or worthless member." Mann conversed privately with Boatright, and offered to help him escape. Boatright grasped the opportunity. Mann asked Moorman's permission to talk with Boatright out of earshot, then shouldered his shotgun and walked toward a canebrake with the prisoner. Suddenly Mann told Boatright to run. But Boatright sprinted only a few steps before Mann emptied the shotgun into his back. Other Regulators, in on the ruse, had their rifles ready and loosed a volley, and Boatright "fell to the earth a mangled corpse." Now only Tiger Jim and Henry Strickland – rumored to be hiding in Louisiana – remained at large from the party that had assassinated Charles Jackson.

Mann soon found himself humiliated by Colonel Moorman in front of fellow Regulators. The company had a rule that the "spoils of war," or property taken from those killed or flogged out of the county, "should be divided equally among the captors." Mann "managed to get possession of" a coat stripped from a hanging victim, perhaps Squire Humphries. Although Mann promised to pay the value of the coat into the treasury, there was little cash in circulation and he did not have "a single dollar." When Moorman next encountered Mann, at a house near Shelbyville, "the Colonel was in an exceedingly bad humor," which brought out his propensity to be a bully. Although a large crowd was present, including several ladies, Moorman brusquely demanded that Mann produce the cash or hand over the coat. Mann made excuses but Moorman harshly insisted, drawing an angry refusal. Moorman exploded into action, beating Mann with the same bois d'arc walking stick he used on Moderators. With ladies and fellow Regulators laughing at his predicament, the bitterly embarrassed Mann surrendered the coat and departed in shame. Later he threatened to join the Moderators and – when Moorman was not present – "lustily swore to be avenged of the indignity."[4]

There was an effort early in 1842 to control the mounting extralegal violence in Shelby County. Judge William B. Ochiltree intended to convene the spring term of Shelby County's district court with the primary intention of securing indictments against men responsible for the hanging of the McFadden brothers. Ochiltree had migrated from Alabama to Texas in 1839 when he was twenty-eight years of age. He opened a law practice in San Augustine. Soon he was appointed judge of the Fifth Judicial District of the Republic of Texas. Judge Ochiltree was aware of the dangerous situation in

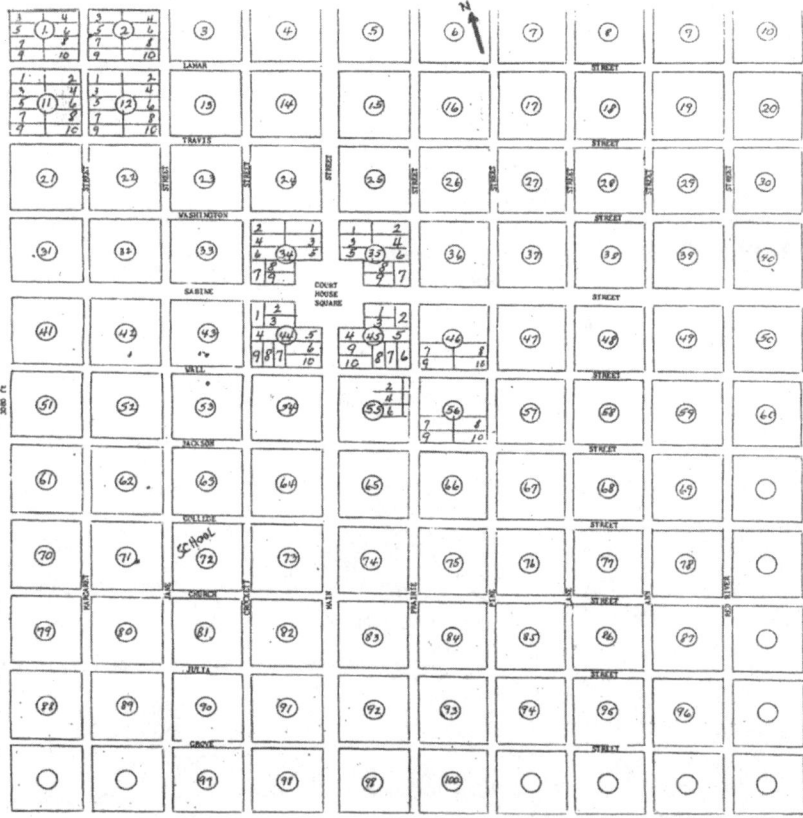

Original plat of Shelbyville. The courthouse square was 250 feet on each side. Main and Sabine streets were 60 feet wide; the other streets were 30 feet wide, and a great many of the throughfares and blocks remained undeveloped. As witth many other town plats, topography was ignored. A tall hill loomed just northeast of the square, and the Shelbyville Cemetery began to grow approximately on Blocks, 5, 6, 15 and 16. *(Plat provided to the author by Johnny Hargrove.)*

Shelby County, as well as of Judge John Hansford's flight from the court at Pulaski the previous summer. But Judge Ochiltree was a far more formidable man than Hansford.[5]

Watt Moorman intended to accomplish in Shelbyville what Charles Jackson had done in Pulaski. "Moorman and his party wanted the court broken up," said Dr. Ashcroft, "and concluded to frighten the judge...off the bench." After court convened on a Monday, a grand jury was impaneled and sworn in, then adjourned until the next morning. When Judge Ochiltree arrived on Tuesday, "a small piece of artillery mounted on cart wheels" had been hauled onto the public square and aimed at the log courthouse.[6]

Judge Ochiltree marched past the cannon and into the courthouse. Mounting his bench, the judge reached beneath his coat, pulled out two pistols, and deliberately placed each gun on the desk before him. The judge had come armed and had made it clear that he would tolerate no disorder. Judge Ochiltree then ordered Sheriff Alfred George to remove the cannon and arrest anyone who interfered. The sheriff, apparently emboldened by the forceful Ochiltree, dealt with the cannon and no one tried to stop him. Instead of being intimidated, Judge Ochiltree had imposed his will on the sheriff, the Regulators, and the assembled crowd.

With court in session, District Attorney Royal T. Wheeler – later a member of the state Supreme Court – presented the grand jury with a list of more than a dozen men "who had been the principal actors in the execution of the McFaddens...." Most if not all of the grand jury members had been part of that crowd when the McFaddens were hanged, since everyone in and around Shelbyville had been present. If grand jury members were present, they had voted for execution, and some may have participated in some way with the proceedings. The daunting presence of Judge Ochiltree suddenly made the authority of the law a tangible threat to lawbreakers. Under the angry glare of the judge, a majority of the grand jury members indicated that they had participated in the McFadden mob and were "incompetent to sit." The grand jury therefore lacked a quorum, and no indictments could be handed down. A disgusted Judge Ochiltree returned to San Augustine.

Despite Ochiltree's impressive performance, the law again

had proved powerless in Shelby County. Deputy Sheriff John Middleton wrote that "about March, 1842, the old troubles were revived by the return of some of the members of the old gang and their waylaying citizens upon the public roads and in the woods." In the atmosphere of renewed lawlessness, Middleton himself became a target of Moderators resentful that he had led the pursuit of the McFadden party. He was stalked by the Strickland brothers, Jack Crane, John Heath, Farrar Metcalf, "and three others whose names I never learned." For a time Middleton eluded "persistent efforts" to assassinate him, but finally he was ambushed near his cabin. On Saturday morning, March 26, 1842, he went into the woods to catch up his horses. Suddenly two Regulators triggered shotgun blasts from concealment. They quickly reloaded and fired again, then fled the scene.[7]

Middleton recounted that "three balls entered my hip, two struck my hand, and one striking the powder horn at my side and going through that gave me a flesh wound. Other balls pierced my clothing in different places."

Middleton limped back to his home. His wife had heard the shotgun blasts and scurried out in search of him. Middleton remembered that "we soon met and returned home." Middleton rode to the cabin of a neighbor, Nathan Matthews, about a mile away. Word of the attack on Middleton spread quickly, and before nightfall fifty Regulators were scouring the countryside for the bushwhackers. Jack Crane was apprehended and brought to Middleton by Elijah Roberts, son of Shelby County pioneer Moses Roberts, but the other suspect could not be found.

After spending a few days with Nathan Matthews, Middleton returned home. But he was anxious to join the manhunt. "I did not permit my wounds to keep me long confined to the house, and on the fifth day I was on horseback and rode in a dark and stormy night fourteen miles in search of the men who attempted my life." Middleton had left his sickbed too soon, and he fell desperately ill. In his disabled condition it was unsafe for him to remain at home, so Middleton was taken to the home of a brother-in-law, fifteen miles south of Shreveport, Louisiana. This time he stayed in bed for five weeks for a full convalescence. When Middleton finally returned home in May, he stayed overnight at Logansport "to avoid another gang lying by the wayside to attack me."

Healed and back home, Middleton learned good news about two of his would-be assassins. "The day after my arrival I received the most welcome information that Jim Strickland and Farrar Metcalf had been lately killed in Louisiana for negro stealing." After the McFadden hangings, Tiger Jim and Henry Strickland established a hideout in Natchitoches Parish, where they were joined by other Shelby County fugitives. These outlaws robbed travelers and stole slaves and planned revenge against Regulators. The Stricklands and Metcalf, among others, reputedly had attempted to waylay John Middleton. Having failed, they returned to Louisiana, where Tiger Jim and Farrar Metcalf tried one robbery too many. "Tiger Jim got his brains blown out," related Eph Daggett.[8]

Henry Strickland fled to Hunt County in North Texas, where he acquired "a fine stud horse" and a race horse. But Henry "could not behave himself long," observed Daggett. In a grocery store, Henry, drunk or angry or both, "was cowing the storekeeper, throwing whiskey all over the house, and raving like a wild animal." When a "Colonel Shoemaker" entered the store carrying his rifle, Henry challenged him to fight. Henry advanced on Shoemaker, who swung his rifle in self-defense. "The lock of the gun entered the brain pan, killing one of the most ferocious men I ever saw." But Daggett added, "Henry was the unluckiest fighter I ever knew."[9]

With Henry Strickland dead, just one member of the Charles Jackson assassination team remained alive. Bledsoe was killed in Montgomery; Buckskin Bill and John McFadden were hanged by a mob at Shelbyville; Squire Humphries was lynched by Regulators; Boatright was shotgunned in the back; Tiger Jim was shot in the head in Louisiana; and Henry Strickland was killed in a brawl. Only young Baily McFadden, pardoned by the Shelbyville mob because of his age, was left standing. There had been a full measure of retribution for Charles Jackson.

Captain Jackson's successor, Colonel Watt Moorman, interrupted his Regulator responsibilities long enough to take a bride. A passionate ladies' man, "Moorman had for some time been paying court to a Miss Daggett," the daughter of a Shelby County farmer and the sister of Regulators Eph and Charles Daggett. Helen Daggett, according to one who knew her, was "universally esteemed, handsome, sprightly, and of strong but wayward passions." Her father, like many other citizens troubled over the lawlessness in Shelby County, regarded Moorman "as a public benefactor whose motives were pure and patriotic, and as one whose services at this important crisis could not be dispensed with."[10]

Helen had a romantic temperament, and "she looked upon Moorman as a brave and chivalrous gentleman." She became "infected with the same general excitement which prevailed throughout the country, and took a deep interest in the tragic and thrilling events then transpiring." Helen saw Moorman almost every day, and responded "to his artful and insinuating attacks upon her affections...." Helen Daggett became Mrs. Watt Moorman.

Eph Daggett had seen a different side of Colonel Moorman: "I was very much opposed to the match." Eph bitterly felt that Moorman "had stolen my sister," and the two men stopped speaking.[11]

At first Moorman treated his bride with kindness and charm. "But in addition to his other vices, he was a gambler, a drunkard, and a libertine," seethed Dr. Ashcroft. "The greater portion of his time was spent away from home, and when he did return, it was only to heap upon her the most heartless abuse." Helen's image of

Helen Daggett Moorman. As a high-spirited young woman, Helen married Watt Moorman and rode as a Regulator scout and decoy. *(Courtesy Shelby County Historical Museum)*

Moorman soon was shattered, but like most wives of the nineteenth century she intended to stay with her marriage. Although Helen was impetuous and had a "fiery temperament," she broke into "tears and entreaties" when Moorman asked for a separation. "She was willing to suffer neglect, coldness, nay, even abuse, so that she was near him." Moorman nevertheless was "inexorable," and Helen reluctantly moved back to her father's farm.[12]

Helen remained captivated by the life-and-death events swirling around her, and she could not shake off her infatuation with Moorman. As wife of the Regulator commander, Helen had briefly experienced the center of Shelby County drama. Still legally married to the Colonel, the high-spirited young woman continued to identify with the Regulator cause. When Regulator-Moderator violence escalated to unprecedented proportions, Helen Daggett Moorman found herself irresistibly drawn to the action.

Surveyors placed this granite marker on the north-south meridian on the boundary between the United States and the Republic of Texas. One side has the letters "R.T.", and this side announced: "MERIDn BOUNDARY ESTABLISHED A.D. 1840". The only original international boundary marker in the contiguous U.S. stands in southeastern Panola County. A larger marker at the nearby Sabine River was the victim of erosion. *(Photo by the author)*

# 7 Of Hogs and Men

*"But we will see that you do your duty. If
you do not by God I'll make you."*
Watt Moorman to Sheriff Lewellyn

During 1841 and 1842 more than fifteen men were slain in Regulator-Moderator violence and others were wounded or flogged. By 1843, with the Moderator company dormant, Regulator activities lessened and a period of comparative tranquility prevailed in Shelby County. "With the exception of caning an occasional Moderator who ventured into the precincts of the company," observed Dr. Ashcroft, "nothing occurred worthy of record."[1]

Then, a killing over stolen hogs revived in full force the murderous passions of the previous two years. Hog stealing was a serious matter. Almost every farmer in East Texas raised hogs and pork in its different forms was the most common meat at settlers' tables. While most farmers raised only enough swine to feed their own households, some raised large herds and drove them down to town for barter or sale. These short-range "pig drives" in East Texas preceded the far longer and more colorful drives of Texas longhorns. As a valuable commodity, hogs were targeted by thieves, and farmers could become just as irate over the theft of hogs as of horses or cattle.

In 1843 hogs were stolen from the farm of Henry Runnels, the man who had pled for the life of young Baily McFadden. Runnels owned land a mile or so north of Shelbyville, and he accused a neighbor, Samuel N. Hall, of stealing his hogs. Although both

Runnels and Hall were Regulators, hog theft superceded political affiliation. Hall "indignantly denied" the accusation, and both men "armed themselves to the teeth," although they prudently avoided a meeting which would result in shooting.[2]

A widower named Stanfield, who apparently worked for Runnels, resided with his children on the Runnels property. Stanfield felt an allegiance toward Runnels, and he too believed that Hall was the hog thief. While drinking heavily one day in Shelbyville, Stanfield encountered Hall. With drunken belligerence, Stanfield accused Hall of stealing the Runnels hogs. Again denying the charge, Hall told Stanfield the matter was none of his business, and that Runnels could do his own fighting. In reply Stanfield produced a pistol "and shot him down in his tracks." The murderer mounted the closest horse and galloped out of town.

Amon Lewellyn, elected sheriff on February 6, 1843[3] "procured a writ," organized a posse, and rode northeastward in hot pursuit. At the Sabine River, swollen from recent rains, the posse found the stolen horse. The fugitive had attempted to cross the river in a small boat, but the oarsman had been forced to turn back because of darkness and dangerous currents. Stanfield insisted on going ashore on an island, saying he would wade and swim to Louisiana. The boatman advised him that he would enter Louisiana in a swamp north of Logansport, but Stanfield was desperate. After Sheriff Lewellyn talked to the boatman, he sent part of his posse down to cross on the Logansport ferry and guard the road. Stanfield managed to cross the river, but after stumbling only half a mile through the swamp, he took refuge in the fork of a tree and began crying for help. Lewellyn's posse could hear his terrified voice.

At daylight, Lewellyn and his remaining men took a boat across the river near a granite boundary marker placed by the Republic of Texas. Ignoring the international border, Sheriff Lewellyn entered the United States intent upon his mission of informal extradition. Penetrating the swamp, Lewellyn and his posse left their boat and tramped toward the sound of Stanfield's cries. They found the fugitive perched miserably in the tree. "He had lost his hat and shoes, and his clothes were completely drenched with muddy water. His teeth chattered and his whole frame shook as though suffering a severe ague...."

Stanfield had spent a wretched night. The sounds of the swamp, the liquor he had consumed, the cold-blooded murder he had committed – all wildly stimulated and tormented his imagination and conscience. He swore "that the ghost of the man he had murdered had been his constant companion through the whole of that long, dark night; that he could see it distinctly amid the gloom, flitting about upon the surface of the mad waters, and occasionally taking its seat close beside him on a limb or log." The ghost "even went so far once or twice... as to lay its cold, icy hand on his shoulder, and commenced chattering to him in a familiar manner." Posse members testified that Stanfield "looked twenty years older than he had the day before."

Stanfield was brought back to Shelbyville and jailed to await the next session of the district court. Someone – perhaps one of his children, on a visit – smuggled a file to the prisoner. He filed through his irons, then used the tool to open the lock on the jail door, probably in the middle of the night. Stanfield escaped Shelbyville and once more headed east, this time hurrying across Louisiana into Mississippi. Once again a criminal had slipped through the legal apparatus of East Texas. But Stanfield would find it easier to escape Shelbyville's small timber lockup than to evade the inexorable spirit of vendetta that pervaded the region.

In the spring of 1844 hired killers rode into Shelby County. William Wells Williams was offered $1,000 to kill Watt Moorman. Williams (an alias) was contacted in March 1844 in the Trinity County community of Alabama by John Haley. Haley owned land about twelve miles east of Shelbyville, but following a clash with Moorman he left Shelby County. Williams could not resist $1,000, so he rode north to Douglass, in Nacogdoches County, where he was told to meet John M. Bradley. In Douglass, Williams met Bradley, along with Joseph Moore, Nat Smythe, Thomas Garner, and two gunmen named Bill York and Ben Hines. Williams was assured by Bradley that he would provide $1,000 for the death of Moorman, as well as sanctuary at his home. Bradley then led the party to his house, ten miles south of Shelbyville on Patroon Creek.[4]

Bradley, in his mid-forties, was rumored to have ridden as a young man with John Murrell's gang. He brought his family to Texas in 1832. Later that year Bradley served as captain of the Tenaha Militia during the Battle of Nacogdoches, then represented the Municipality of Tenaha at the Convention of 1832 at San Felipe. When the Texas Revolution erupted in 1835, he raised a company and marched to San Antonio, where he participated in the Grass Fight and in the ensuing siege. The following spring Captain Bradley commanded a company of cavalry during the climactic campaign of the Texas Revolution. Back in Shelby County, he remarried, expanded his land holdings, and "was accused of keeping a public house for the accommodation of horse thieves and dealers in bogus money." During the Regulator-Moderator War, threats "freely passed" between Bradley and Moorman. With his martial background, Bradley continually urged the Moderators to mobilize in force. When the Moderators refused to reorganize their company, Bradley and other men pledged a fund to be used to hire killers. Eph Daggett understood that gunmen were imported to kill "eight or nine Regulators. They were to receive $1000 for Watt Moorman, $700 for John F. Myrick, $500 for old man Runnels and so on down the line." John Middleton stated that William Wells Williams, Ben Hines, Bill York, and James Seekers were hired to "kill seventeen men, and those the most prominent in the county."[5]

After spending a night at Bradley's house, Williams rode into Shelbyville, where he was approached by Amos and Joe Hall, two of the surviving brothers of Samuel Hall. The Hall brothers told Williams that they knew why he was in Shelby County, but "that it was impossible to get Moorman...." Instead, they offered him $500 to kill Henry Runnels, who had "hired one Stanfield to kill another brother of theirs, and ...had been the cause of death of many good and honest men...." Williams agreed and was directed to the cabin of William Todd, three miles south of Shelbyville, where

"Amos Hall came and paid me the sum of forty dollars as part of the reward."[6]

Ben Hines also was assigned to the Runnels killing. Within a few days Hines and Williams rode to the Runnels home and told Henry they were hunting stolen horses. They described their non-existent horses and asked Henry to keep an eye out for them. They accepted overnight hospitality, and learned that within a few days Runnels intended to deliver a load of cotton to Shreveport. The next day Hines decided he could not kill a man who had shown him such courtesy; he left Shelby County and was not seen again.

Although his accomplice had departed, Williams now knew what his intended victim looked like. He rode south to John Bradley's place, where he was introduced to James Seekers, alias James Smyth, the fourth hired gunman. Seekers had been assigned by Samuel Todd to kill John Myrick, who had taken a keelboat down the Sabine, but the assassin was unable to get a good shot from the riverbank. The Hall brothers, in another meeting at Samuel Todd's, persuaded Williams and Seekers to go after Runnels on the road to Shreveport. John Bradley gave Seekers a double-barreled shotgun, and when the two assassins stopped by Jim Hall's farm, Williams also was given a shotgun.[7]

When Runnels headed for Shreveport with one or more cotton wagons (he had stored his cotton beneath a shed since the previous fall), he was accompanied by his son, Stephen, and a few slaves. After ferrying across the Sabine, Runnels led his party another eight miles before camping for the night. After feeding his horses, Henry reclined at the foot of a post oak tree. At this point, Seekers and Williams rode past. Stephen recognized Williams and told his father, who called the travelers over. Henry asked Williams if he had found the stolen horses, then offered them supper as well as corn and fodder for their mounts.

Williams and Seekers remained mounted during the conversation, with their guns resting across the pommels of their saddles. Suddenly, treacherously, Seekers raised his double-barreled shotgun and blasted Henry in the chest. Runnels died instantly.

The assassins wheeled their horses and galloped away, but in his haste, Williams rode beneath a limb. Knocked from his horse, Williams scrambled to escape on foot, leaving his gun and hat behind. Seekers quickly disappeared down the road.

The body of Henry Runnels was taken home. The next day Stephen Runnels and several men returned to the murder site, retrieved Williams' gun, and picked up the trail. The Runnels posse found Williams at a cabin about twenty-five miles from the murder scene on the road toward Natchitoches. Runnels and his men surrounded the cabin, and at dawn Williams emerged carrying a gun. He faced an array of gun muzzles and an order to surrender. The people inside quickly left the cabin while a parley took place. Stephen Runnels courageously advanced, and when he was within ten feet, Williams dropped his gun and declared, "I never killed your father nor no other man."[8]

Williams was brought back to Texas and placed in a blockhouse three miles east of Shelbyville built by Matthew Brinson.[9] A dozen armed men guarded the cabin. Meanwhile, Watt Moorman had led a posse of Regulators southeast to East Hamilton, thinking that at the local ferry Seekers might try to cross the Sabine back into Texas. Moorman missed Seekers, so he led his men back to Shelbyville. But Seekers, anticipating that the ferry landing at East Hamilton would be under guard, engaged the ferryman to take him in a skiff to the Texas side at a bluff some distance away. The ferryman knew nothing of the most recent murder, and Seekers pawned the gun given to him by Bradley to pay his ferriage. Seekers made his way through the woods about ten miles to the home of John Bradley on Patroon Creek. Bradley, an old hand at helping men on the run, provided Seekers with a horse and helped him escape to western Texas.[10]

When Watt Moorman arrived back in Shelbyville, Williams was brought before the Regulators for an interrogation that served as his only trial. He was told that if he would confess his guilt and reveal the names of those who had hired the killers, his life would be spared. Williams claimed to have told Seekers that "he could not shoot a man who had shown so much kindness as Runnels had at his house and again at the camp." Seekers supposedly reported, "I am going to have that money and kill a damned Regulator and a man who either killed his neighbor or had it done." Williams revealed that John Bradley "had a big sum of money made up to have a lot of men killed in Shelbyville," starting with Watt Moorman, John Myrick, and "old man Runnels." The Hall brothers, continued Williams, were willing to put up $500 for the death of Runnels, while "other prominent men" offered rewards for several proposed victims. The highest bounty, $1000, was placed on Moorman's head.[11]

Moorman was incensed. A search of Williams turned up about twenty silver dollars, which Moorman distributed among the Regulators who were present. Then he asked for a vote on the fate of Williams. Despite the promise made to the prisoner, the Regulators voted unanimously for hanging. Parson William Blackburn agreed to erect a gallows on the public square.

The gallows went up about fifty feet from the courthouse, and the next day, Wednesday, May 8, 1844, a large crowd gathered for the hanging of the "notorious hired assassinator." Hangings were public entertainments, and a number of men drank heavily. On the scaffold Williams "was cool and collected to the last," admired an onlooker, "and only regretted ever having associated himself with bad men, and charged his misfortunes to the miserable habit of gambling." He refused to disclose his real name "because I will not bring disgrace on my father's family." He handed the hangman "a fine gold ring" to be sent to a young lady in Mississippi.

The doomed man asked Pastor Blackburn to sell his horse and provide him a decent burial with the proceeds. But Blackburn kept the horse for himself, gave a slave the dead man's boots as payment for digging a shallow grave, and had Williams buried in a pine box in his clothes rather than a shroud. Dr. Ashcroft was skeptical that Parson Blackburn would "ever get to heaven," and he also doubted that the gold ring was sent to Mississippi.[12]

After the hanging, Colonel Moorman called his Regulator

company together and vowed that the gallows should remain standing until every man who had been implicated had been taken into custody and hanged. "A troop of men, some half drunk," was dispatched to arrest Joseph Hall, according to Eph Daggett, who rode with them. Hall lived only a mile north of town, and the Regulator riders soon surrounded his cabin. Hall gave himself up without resistance, but his wife insisted on accompanying him into town, where preparations already were being made for another hanging. Hall was related by marriage to the Dial family, and he was taken to the Dial Hotel on the square.

"The excitement was high when Hall got to the Hotel," remembered Daggett. When presented with the accusations of Williams, Hall declared the statement "all false, and he appealed to every reasonable man to look at the thing reasonably." Hall denied any collaboration with John Bradley, reminding the crowd that he and Bradley had clashed years earlier and had not spoken since. He was aware of the "fuss about hogs" between his brother and Henry Runnels, and admitted that his deceased brother had a quarrelsome nature. Hall adamantly declared that he had never seen Seekers and Williams. Mrs. Hall began to weep and plead for the life of her husband. A number of Regulators were moved by her tearful supplications, and "they were not prepared to murder a woman's husband while she stood by," observed Dr. Ashcroft. Approached by "many of his followers," Moorman reluctantly consented to suspend the lynching. Hall was taken before a justice of the peace, bound over to answer the charges against him at the next district court, then released on bond.[13]

Joseph Hall received information that Stanfield, the jail escapee who had murdered his brother on behalf of Henry Runnels, was in Mississippi. Joseph's matter-of-fact acceptance of his brother's death in front of the Regulator inquisitors was only a performance. Blood called to blood, and Joseph burned to avenge his brother Samuel. Enlisting one of the Dials, who had married into the Hall family, Joseph rode to the Mississippi location where Stanfield supposedly had fled. There Hall and Dial learned that their prey had moved to Arkansas. The two pursuers rode to the Arkansas neighborhood where Stanfield was reported, and they began to shadow him. They jumped Stanfield on a lonely stretch of road, bound him, and spirited him away. One man led Stanfield's horse while the other rode behind to block any escape attempt. They pushed on through the night, covering fifty miles before stopping for the day in a secluded thicket.[14]

Dial procured food at a nearby house, and after returning he had to persuade Hall not to shoot their prisoner. After dark the party again mounted up, and during the night they crossed the Arkansas line into the Cherokee Nation, in Indian Territory. At daybreak they left the trail and rode deep into a rocky, timbered ravine. About a mile into the isolated gorge, Hall and Dial stopped and prepared to hang their captive. Stanfield begged to be taken back to Shelbyville, claiming that he was willing to die by the hands of the law. "But, oh, do not take my life and leave me here, in this dark and gloomy spot, to become food for wild beasts."

That fate was exactly Hall's idea of a suitable vengeance for the life of his brother. A rope was tossed over the limb of a tree and noosed around Stanfield's neck. His horse was slapped, and after he died, Hall and Dial left his corpse dangling from the tree. The avengers rode back toward Texas leading Stanfield's gray horse – which they assumed was stolen. Soon after returning home, Hall, realizing that his life was at great risk in Shelby County, forfeited his bond and moved away with his wife.[15]

Four men now had died in the wake of the theft of Henry Runnels' hogs, including Runnels himself. Two were shot in cold blood and two were hanged. These murderous events reawakened, late in 1843, the Regulator-Moderator furies of 1841 and 1842.

Colonel Watt Moorman and his Regulators now felt a renewed sense of purpose. Riders were sent "to prowl about the country" in search of men implicated by Williams, but no one was found in the countryside. Instead, Sam Todd, Amos Hall, and John Bradley forted up in Bradley's house ten miles south of Shelbyville. Bradley had tried to galvanize fellow Moderators into action by arranging the assassination of leading Regulators. Todd had been accused of attempting to have Myrick killed, although Todd and Myrick were known to be friends, and many people did not believe Williams' accusation. Amos Hall, like his brother, had been a Regulator. But Regulators had tried to hang Joseph Hall, and now they were hunting Amos – who switched sides and became a Moderator. The Bradley house was fortified and stocked with guns, ammunition, and provisions, and the Regulators had no stomach for a frontal assault on this stronghold.[16]

Watt Moorman's frustration mounted. Amos Hall and John Bradley, who had offered $1,000 for his death, had secured themselves. Joseph Hall had been within his grasp but the pleas of his wife had helped the man escape hanging, and now he had fled the country. Moorman therefore targeted James Hall, who worked a modest farm a few miles northeast of Shelbyville. Hall's labor supported a wife and several children, as well as the fifth brother, John Hall, who was simple-minded. Moorman wanted to execute James on the gallows in Shelbyville, but the hanging of Williams aroused public opinion "against such proceedings." So Moorman – somehow reasoning that an ambush would be more acceptable – sent a squad of gunmen to Hall's farm. James, assisted by John, was plowing a corn field. The assassins concealed themselves in bushes beside the split-rail fence. When James came near, "a volley of buckshot was discharged at him, and he fell between the plow handles...." The plow horse bolted, and the gunmen fled. Mrs. Hall ran into the field, finding her husband bleeding and in agony. James died within a few hours, but he and John recognized two or three of the assassins. Eventually Stephen Runnels was indicted for the murder, but in court John Hall became so confused by defense counsel that his testimony was discounted and the defendant was acquitted.[17]

"The murder of Hall created a deep sensation in the community," recalled Dr. Ashcroft. Many of the Regulators were "shocked and astonished" because Moorman had not consulted the members about killing Hall. Although all Regulators were blamed, "the murder was not even canvassed, much less agreed upon by the company...."[18]

John Bradley, still confined to his stronghold on Patroon Creek, made another effort to rally the Moderators. Bradley repeatedly had encouraged his friends to take up arms against the Regulators, but the Moderator faction refused to reorganize. Attempting to work through Shelby County's feeble legal system, Bradley arranged for attorneys and Justice of the Peace Thomas Lister to prepare writs of arrest for Watt Moorman and several Regulators. These writs were given by Justice of the Peace Lister to Sheriff Lewellyn, who now faced the daunting task of trying to arrest and hold Moorman. Before acting on the arrest documents, Sheriff Lewellyn quietly notified Moorman and the others, who "requested two or three days to consider the matter and consult with their friends." The sheriff, who had only one deputy, felt compelled to oblige them. Moorman promptly summoned fifty Regulators "and commanded them to remain under arms in the town of Shelbyville until further orders." Sheriff Lewellyn countered by assembling about the same number of armed men at the Todd blockhouse – a posse that was the first large mustering of the Moderator faction in two years. The public feared that a "war of extermination" was about to erupt.[19]

Sheriff Lewellyn asked for a truce, and two days later he received word from Moorman that if he and one other man would come unarmed into town, the accused Regulators would submit to arrest. Courageously, Lewellyn and Deputy Jeff Cravens rode into Shelbyville and faced more than half a hundred armed Regulators. True to their word, Moorman and his friends submitted to Lewellyn's custody, demanding a speedy trial. They arrogantly refused to be tried under Justice of the Peace Lister, insisting that their cases be heard under Justice of the Peace John Ingram, a fellow Regulator: "before him and no one else they agreed to appear." Predictably, Ingram's court was a farce. The lawyers retained by Bradley were warned not to come to court and wisely were absent from the proceedings. Justice Ingram examined the writs and declared "that they were defective and had been illegally issued." Court was adjourned, and the freed Regulators crossed the square to the Doggery, a grog shop where they "imbibed a quantity of liquor suitable to the joyous occasion."[20]

Sheriff Lewellyn and Deputy Cravens rode back to the Moderator camp on the Todd place, where the posse awaited news of the court. Shortly after Lewellyn began relating the legal maneuvers, a rider arrived to deliver writs from Justice Ingram for the sheriff charging John Bradley, Amos Hall, and Samuel Todd as accessories to the murder of Henry Runnels. The writs were accompanied by a letter from Moorman to the sheriff:

Shelbyville, Texas

A. Lewellyn,
Sir – You have been so damned energetic in attempting to enforce the laws of the country I herewith forward you writs

Greek Revival residence built in 1839 in San Augustine by Stephen W. Blount, a signer of the Texas Declaration of Independence. *(Photo by the author)*

Greek Revival residence built in San Augustine in 1839 by Ezekial Cullen. Other Greek Revival houses were erected, and the additional presence of churches and a "university" helped earn San Augustine the title "Athens of Texas." *(Photo by the author)*

against your particular friends Bradley, Todd and Hall. We will now see if you are as persevering in the discharge of your duty as you have recently been. But we will see that you do your duty.

*C. W. Moorman*[21]

Bradley, Todd, and Hall engaged Dr. Ashcroft and another lawyer as counsel. Reversing the strategic precedent set by Moorman -- who refused a summons to appear in court – the accused insisted on being heard before Justice Lister. The attorneys moved that since Runnels was murdered in Louisiana, the court's "jurisdiction did not extend beyond the limits of the Republic." Lister upheld the motion and the accused were discharged. Bradley correctly assumed that Regulators would try to ambush him on his way home, so he abandoned the road and slipped through the back country to his fortified house.[22]

Moorman continued to threaten Bradley's life. Bradley replied with threats of his own, but neither he nor a hired assassin had much hope of penetrating Moorman's bodyguard of Regulators. During the summer of 1844, Bradley left his wife and children at their home and went to San Augustine for a cooling-off period. Known as the "Athens of Texas," San Augustine boasted churches and a college and Greek Revival homes. A system of courts and law enforcement officers was in place. Bradley could lead life in the open on the streets of San Augustine, while his home on Patroon Creek was less than ten miles away. Bradley lodged at Berry's Hotel, but carried a double-barreled shotgun everywhere he went.[23]

In July 1844, hearing rumors that his principal foe had left Shelby County for San Augustine, Moorman dispatched John Farrar to try to find him. As he neared San Augustine, Farrar encountered Bradley on horseback. Bradley alertly leveled his shotgun and asked if he was John Farrar the Regulator. Farrar claimed to be John's brother Frank, from Arkansas. Bradley told Farrar to look down the barrel of his gun and asked him if he saw anything. Farrar said that he did not. "Well," Bradley replied ominously, "there are twenty-five buckshot down there concealed

Famed Texas Ranger captain and Civil War officer John S. "Rip" Ford (1815-1897). As a young man, Dr. Ford was a San Augustine physician and lawyer, and he conversed with John Bradley shortly before the latter's murder. *(Courtesy Western History Collections, University of Oklahoma Library)*

under a wad, and if I ever discover that you have deceived me I will certainly lodge them all in your carcass."[24]

Permitted to resume his journey, Farrar left the road after a short distance, fearful that he might be followed. Soon lost in the forest, it took him two days to reach Shelbyville, normally a distance of eighteen miles. After learning of the chance encounter with Bradley, Moorman "laughed at Farrar for being a silly coward." Then the Regulator leader picked four or five men and rode south, camping near San Augustine. The Regulators were armed with shotguns, bowie knives, and new Colt five-shooters.

A "protracted meeting" was being conducted by a Baptist minister in San Augustine before large crowds every night. Services were being held in the Masonic hall two blocks east of the courthouse square. On Saturday night Bradley was in attendance, and so was his ever-present shotgun. Facing north, the front of the hall featured a gallery (or porch), large columns, and two sets of doors. On the gallery Bradley visited with Dr. John S. Ford, before taking a seat

In 1844, Regulator leader Watt Moorman murdered John Bradley as he left a Baptist service being held in San Augustine's Masonic hall on this site. A second lodge hall was built there in 1910. *(Photo by the author)*

toward the rear.

The Regulators slipped into town and Moorman left his men with the horses while he walked to the Masonic hall. A shotgun would have attracted attention to a stranger, so Moorman's principal weapon was a pistol. On a hot July night the doors were flung open, and the gallery was crowded with slaves peering inside. From the edge of the gallery Moorman spotted Bradley. When the crowd emerged at the end of the service, Moorman edged near Bradley, pulled his weapon, and fired a pistol ball into his stomach. Bradley reflexively triggered one barrel of his shotgun, but the weapon must have been pointed downward, because no one was hit.

Bradley collapsed, stricken with a mortal wound. A woman knelt beside him "and prayed most fervently." The startling sound of gunshots at a religious service triggered instant pandemonium. There were screams, a couple of ladies went into hysterics, and two or three others thought they were wounded. In the confusion Bradley walked away from the Masonic hall toward the horses. But Justice of the Peace A.B. Patton saw the pistol fired and followed Moorman. Patton told Moorman he was under arrest, but he heard the click of a pistol hammer inside Watt's coat, then the other Regulators materialized from the darkness. Patton made a quick decision and extended his hand. "I'm your friend, Col. Moorman. Good night."[25]

While Moorman and his friends rode off into the night, Bradley was carried to his boarding house. Doctors came to his bedside, but could do little. Bradley suffered intensely through the night, repeatedly muttering that if Moorman had given him "an equal chance" then he would have been "satisfied to meet his end." At dawn Bradley asked to be turned onto his side, remarking to those around him "that he had been basely murdered by a scoundrel, but wanted them to tell his family and friends that he had died like a brave man." These were Bradley's last words. His remains were taken back to Shelby County for burial near his home.[26]

"The character of Bradley presented a strange medley of contradictions...," wrote Dr. Ashcroft, who had observed the man closely. Dr. Ashcroft penned a eulogy of sorts. Bradley "was a kind parent, a good husband, and an obliging man; but yet he was known to be connected with men banded together to swindle and defraud the public, in various ways. He possessed many traits of the noblest nature but they were so blackened by the reflection of his vices as to be almost entirely obscured."[27]

By the next morning Moorman and his squad were back in Shelby County with the main body of Regulators. There were shouts of rejoicing at the news that Colonel Moorman had slain John Bradley. Word spread quickly, and throughout the day more Regulators and Regulator sympathizers came to camp to congratulate Moorman and to join the celebration. An enormous pound cake was concocted. "It was baked in a ten gallon wash kettle with a tube in the center," described Regulator Eph Daggett. "It was covered with several oven lids and baked with a slow fire until it was done through and through." A crowd of two hundred and fifty men shared the cake that night, along with liquid refreshment.[28]

Watt Moorman had pulled off a remarkable coup. The Regulator leader had left the comparative security of Shelby County, then single-handedly stalked his principal nemesis, who was armed with a shotgun. The commander of the Regulators personally had killed the most prominent individual of the opposing faction. This bold stroke was expected to break the back of the Moderators and end serious conflict. But the recent public hanging, the assassination of James Hall at his plow, and now the killing of John Bradley at a church service created a sudden wave of resistance to the Regulators. Shortly after the death of Bradley, Shelby County found itself facing armed strife on a scale that would eclipse any previous fighting.

Eph Daggett, shown here as a prominent founder of Fort Worth. As a younger man, Daggett was a stalwart Regulator, and he left an important first-person account of the East Texas conflict. *(Courtesy Fort Worth Public Library)*

# 8 Mobilization

*"There were no neutral men; there
were no halfway grounds."*
Eph Daggett

Secret meetings were held across Shelby County during July 1844 by those who "had seen enough of mob law...." Moderators long had been disorganized, and in the absence of an effective legal system they were powerless against Watt Moorman's company. While the citizens of Shelbyville "were pretty equally divided between the two parties," armed Regulators controlled the town. Dr. Ashcroft, a Moderator partisan who lived in Shelbyville, stated that overbearing Regulators "treated the Moderators and citizens who visited town with such gross and causeless injustice and hardship that forbearance ceased to be a virtue." Forbearance vanished as Moderators no longer were willing to "submit tamely" to Regulator oppression. American pioneers in East Texas or in any other frontier would never submit to anything for long. Moderators met and found themselves again ready to organize an armed force; many "of the more impetuous and excitable" vehemently urged "that every Regulator in the country should be put to death without quarter."[1]

A day was agreed upon, and about fifty armed men rode from various directions to Bell's Spring, about six miles from Shelbyville. A company was organized, the "Reformers of Shelby County." But the Regulator-Moderator lines had been drawn too deeply for far too long, and everyone ignored the term "Reformers" and called the new organization the Moderators. The Reformers/ Moderators elected as "Commandant" attorney James Jeff Cravens, who had proved his mettle as Sheriff Lewellyn's deputy. Since the Regulators were commanded by a colonel, the Reformer/Moderator leader likewise was designated "Colonel" Cravens.[2]

Colonel Cravens acted decisively. Early the next morning he led his company out of camp, and by nine o'clock half a hundred determined men rode into Shelbyville. The meetings had remained secret, so Colonel Moorman was completely unaware of the formation of the new company and only a handful of Regulators remained in town. When they saw Deputy Sheriff Jeff Cravens thundering into Shelbyville at the head of a column of riders carrying rifles and shotguns, they quickly slipped out of town.

Watt Moorman was enraged that the Moderator faction had seized the county seat. Part of his angry frustration was at his own carelessness. Moorman "gave vent to his wrath in a volley of curses, so remarkable for vindictiveness and profanity, that those who heard him never forgot his language." With his wrath vented, Colonel Moorman sent riders to announce a Regulator rendezvous at a point several miles from Shelbyville. The Regulators gathered in force, and within a few days Colonel Moorman led his men into the county seat. But Colonel Cravens, having demonstrated his new force, had abandoned the town and withdrawn to the countryside, where new men were enlisting by the day. Colonel Moorman also remained only briefly in Shelbyville, before leading the Regulators into camp two miles outside town at Graham's Springs. The opposing camps were only three miles apart. Moorman's ranks swelled to more than 100 men, and both companies prepared for a major clash, gathering supplies and ammunition and provender for their horses.[3]

At this point, "Col. Ashton, Maj. Edwards and others of high standing who were not in any manner identified with either party, offered their services as mediators...." These peacemakers called upon Colonel Moorman in the Regulator camp. He conferred with his men, then provided a note:

Camp Graham Springs, July 1844
I, Charles W. Moorman, Colonel Commandant of the Shelby Guards in behalf of said Guards pledge myself on condition that the men under the command of Col. Cravens

retires to their homes, lays down their arms as quiet and peaceable citizens; that no good citizen within the bounds of the county of Shelby shall be molested.

*C. W. Moorman,* Col. Commandant
S. Guards[4]

The mediators received Moorman's good-will gesture on Sunday, July 21, and took the note to the Moderator camp. Colonel Cravens read Moorman's communication to his men, and following discussion the Moderators agreed to a truce. Cravens and the mediators drew up a document which, in emphasizing the purity of Moderator motives, disavowed "The Secret Machinations & Clandestine Operations of John M Bradley and his accomplices." The Moderators offered unanimous approval, then left for their homes, while the mediators returned to the Regulator camp with the draft:

## THE REPUBLIC OF TEXAS
## COUNTY OF SHELBY

July 24, 1844

Whereas the present Moderating Company did assemble themselves together with the avowed intention or object of suppressing regulating and that the Regulators have since in protection and in defense of themselves concentrated their forces – And that whereas a large portion of the present Moderating Company are good and Reputable Citizens – and have sought refuge in the present Moderating Company for the protection of their lives, and having been seduced into it by false Representations – The Secret Machinations & Clandestine Operations of John M Bradley and his accomplices, and contrary to their knowledge of the fact &

And whereas –a truce to the hostilities of the two Contending parties now and for a time past was concluded on the 21st Inst for the purpose of an amicable arrangement of the differences, and the same having been made the subject of the most Serious Consideration of the Regulating Company – have adopted the following articles as the result of their deliberations

Art Ist That the good citizens of the present Moderating Company – Who have sought refuge among them under a delusion and having Solely for their object the defense and protection of their lives and having Been Seduced into it by false representation, Being convinced that the Causes have not nor do not exist – are respectfully requested to withdraw – and we the Regulators do pledge our lives our liberties & our Sacred honours to adhere strictly to any pretensions or appearances given to any and all Such members of the present Moderating Company –

Art 2nd That all such members of the present Moderating Company – do by these presents disclaim any intention or design to molest or in any manner disturb the peace, tranquility, or quiet of the community – And we the Regulators pledge themselves not to molest or disturb any good and unoffending Citizen, Nor to act on any occasion on mere Rumour or report –

Art 3rd That the parties further agree and bind themselves as Citizens of the Common Community and entitled to equal rights and privileges and immunities under the Constitution and Laws of the Country, to hold themselves amenable and responsible at the Bar of Justice as well as that of Public Opinion for all their future actions

The foregoing has been unanimously adopted by the Regulating Company --

*C. W. Moorman*
Col Comdt of the
Regulating Company

Adopted unanimously
by the Company

*Jas J Cravens*
Col Comdt of the
Reformers of Shelby
County Texas[5]

The Regulators also approved unanimously, and Watt Moorman provided his signature. While most of the Regulators went their separate ways, Moorman kept fifteen or twenty armed men with him.

The truce proved fleeting. For two years Watt Moorman had defined himself as the bold, fearless leader of mounted Regulators, and he could not give up the role. He summoned another dozen or so men, and at the head of thirty Regulators, Colonel Moorman rode to the house of Samuel Todd. Arriving at noon, the Regulators arrested Todd and a young farmhand named Holt who had come in for lunch. Moorman detailed half of his men to escort the prisoners to Matthew Brinson's, while he led the other Regulators to the nearby cabin of seventy-year-old Charles Lindsey. The old man was barefoot on a hot July day, and he was ordered to put on his shoes and catch up his horse. Lindsey thought he was about to be hanged – Todd probably thought the same – and he defiantly refused to cooperate. He would not put on his shoes and he declined to go after his horse, muttering that they recently had hanged a man – Williams – and taken his horse, and he did not want Parson Blackburn to have a Lindsey mount. "You can't cheat me out of many days anyway, you d—d cutthroats, and I don't intend that you should rob me of anything more than enough to pay for the rope."[6]

Lindsey trudged slowly alongside the horseman. A Regulator named Lagon impatiently told the old man if he did not hurry he would cut his suspender with a rifle ball. During the fighting to come, Lagon would have his own suspender cut by a rifle ball, poetic justice with fatal results. At Brinson's place the prisoners were interrogated about the new Moderator company, but they revealed little about who had helped Jeff Cravens organize the Regulator opponents. Although Lindsey had helped reorganize the Moderators, and had ridden triumphantly, along with his son, into Shelbyville behind Colonel Cravens, he was mute on the subject.

Instead of being hanged, the three prisoners were released before sundown. But throughout the afternoon news of the seizure of Lindsey, Todd, and Holt was spread across Shelby County. No sooner had the Regulators left Todd's home with their prisoners, than Todd's daughter saddled up and rode to a neighboring cabin. There "a young man was immediately mounted on a fleet horse and dispatched to spread the news," reported Dr. Ashcroft. Soon there were many Paul Reveres galloping through the countryside. "Every spare horse was put in requisition – before night there was scarcely a family in the county who had not received the intelligence."[7]

Everyone feared that Lindsey, Todd, and Holt would be lynched by the Regulators. Dr. Ashcroft remembered a sudden "reign of terror. All of those who had ever said anything against Moorman and his friends... expected to be dealt with in a similar manner." Neighbors gathered together to fort up at someone's cabin, and other people left their homes to spend the night in the woods. Jeff Cravens and members of his Moderator company realized that they had been taken for fools – Moorman never had intended to abide by the truce. Cravens hastily reorganized the Moderators, including many new recruits.

"There were no neutral men; there were no halfway grounds," related Regulator Eph Daggett. Now the Moderators, too, were under arms, and hunting/sniping blinds began to be found near the homes of Regulators. Farmers stopped working in their fields for fear of ambush, and men took the unusual precaution of barring their doors at night. "No one felt safe."[8]

Both factions recruited in Harrison County, and Regulator John Middleton said that Moderators sent recruiters into Arkansas and Louisiana. Middleton believed that a "company of Arkansas men" had come to Shelby County "to kill me and Howell Hudson." Hudson was informed by friends two days before the killing was rumored to take place. Hudson and half a dozen other Regulators rode to Middleton's cabin, about fifteen miles north of Shelbyville. Middleton's family left that night for safety, but he could not travel without help because his hip wounds had not healed. Instead, his friends concealed him near the road "to intercept the spy of the moderators that night...." The spy "was never discovered," but after dark a "gang" broke into his home. Finding the cabin empty, they apparently feared an ambush and fled into the Tenaha Swamp, floundering desperately in the darkness.[9]

That summer, at a Regulator meeting, John Middleton offered a proposal that would help facilitate the growing ambition of Watt Moorman. "I made a motion that the different counties of the Republic be notified of what was going on with us and advised to organize, arm and protect themselves," related Middleton. "The letters were written by Colonel Moorman and C.T. Hilliard, and being received by these counties had a strong effect." The "strong effect" included the organization of Regulator companies in San Augustine, Nacogdoches, Panola, and Sabine counties.[10]

Redmon and Sarah Choate (center, in old age) moved to Shelby County to Tennessee, where their son, Squire, was a physician. Before his parents departed for Texas, Squire Choate taught his mother as much medicine as he could. In Shelby County Sarah Choate became known as a healer, and during the Regulator-Moderator War she treated wounded men from both factions. When the fighting continued, the Choates moved from their Sabine River headright nearly thirty miles to the northwest and built this dogtrot log cabin atop a hill, raising the younger members of their 13 children there. *(Courtesy Shelby County Historical Museum)*

Colonel Moorman, already commander of the "United Regulating Forces of Harrison, Panola and Shelby Counties," now envisioned county after county sending companies to swell his army. Moorman's "Regulating Forces" would be larger than any other army in the Republic of Texas. Like Haden Edwards and Dr. James Long and other filibusters who had dreamed of seizing control of Mexican Texas, Watt Moorman "now fondly imagined that the auspicious moment had arrived which was to place him in the proud position then occupied by General Houston." Colonel Moorman began to see himself as General Moorman or President Moorman. He confided this dream to his most trusted followers, and selected twelve men who would govern Texas as a Provisional Committee until "a new constitution should be ordained and established." Colonel Leonard Straw was elected president of the committee; Moorman served as commander-in-chief of the military -- and presumably as president after the new constitution was in place."[11]

The Provisional Committee "held a council" at Matthew Brinson's blockhouse on Sunday, July 28, 1844. Colonel Moorman guarded the committee meeting with 100 riders. Colonel Straw stated ominously "that while certain men lived in the county there could be no permanent peace." Watt Moorman stood on a log and addressed his men. He agreed with Straw "that some men must leave the country...." Moorman wanted a list proscribed of men who would be notified "to leave the Republic...." The matter was debated, and several veteran Regulators voiced opposition. "I made a talk against the measure that said that most of the proscribed were Moderators with family ties, and were good average citizens," said Eph Daggett.[12]

"By imprudence and rashness you have lost old Uncle Jimmy Truitt and all his sons and their influence," proclaimed M.T. Johnson. "They were once good Regulators and are now in the Moderator ranks." The entire Truitt clan had been driven by Regulator excesses into the opposite faction. Alfred Truitt married the widow of Joseph Goodbread, who had been murdered by Shelby County's original Regulator, Charles Jackson. Johnson believed that a proscribed list would strengthen Moderator resolve. "I fear the consequences and it is a bad move."[13]

"But Moorman carried with a yell," related Daggett, adding that the "young men all sided with Watt." A committee commanded by Captain Joe Smith was appointed to notify the proscribed men, and a list of twenty-five of "the best fighters on the Moderator's side" was prepared, headed by Sheriff Lewellyn and Colonel Cravens:[14]

Sheriff Amon Lewellyn
John Haley
Richard Haley
Thomas Haley
Allen Haley
Mark Haley
David Strickland
Isaac Strickland
Jonathan Anderson
Isaac Hall
Everett J. Ritter
M.H. Mosley
J.D. Rains

Colonel Jeff Cravens
Samuel Todd
William Todd
Charles Lindsey
James Thomas
W.J. Thomas
Joshua English
John Choate
Harris Davis
Moses F. Wooten
Laurel Long
James West

Watt Moorman directed Captain Smith and his committee to make it clear to each man on the list that if he failed to comply with the decree "he would be considered an outlaw and hung without judge or jury." Moorman believed that if the Regulators could force twenty-five prominent landholders and Moderators out of the country, then other Moderators could be proscribed until no one was left to oppose him. If Moorman could seize absolute control of Shelby County, then larger ambitions were possible. As Moorman began to envision presiding over a greater stage, the fifteen-man Regulator committee rode out of camp on Monday, July 29, to notify Moderator Thomas Haley that he must abandon his home.[15]

Haley, the first man on the list to be so notified, was gathering his hay crop, assisted by several neighbors. Moderators had decided it was not "safe for one man to be found alone." The Regulator committee left the road and approached the Haley cabin from the rear to scout the gathering of men. Concealed in the woods about 150 yards from the cabin, they were discovered by Mrs. Haley, who hurried back to tell her husband. Haley took his rifle, which was charged with two balls, into the stable, and his friends stationed themselves nearby. The mood of these men was belligerent, and Haley decided to fire the first shot. Taking aim at a dark shape in the brush, he carefully squeezed the trigger. The dark shape was Charley Mann's horse, and the animal's jugular vein was severed by a rifle ball. The other bullet passed over the unlucky horse and broke the arm of a mounted Regulator. A long-range "cussing match" ensued, while the horseless Mann clambered up behind one of his friends. "That stopped any further notification," observed Eph Daggett, and the Regulators rode away in "precipitate retreat."[16]

Back at the Regulator camp at Brinson's blockhouse, Captain Smith and his committee reported to Colonel Moorman. The committee members claimed "that they had been repulsed by at least twenty men who were strongly fortified in Haley's stable" and they had no intention of risking their lives on any further notification missions to Moderator strongholds. The Moderators clearly were aroused to the point of organized resistance. After a hasty consultation, the Regulators decided to post a handbill on the courthouse door commanding the listed Moderators "to leave within fifteen days under the prescribed penalty."[17]

By Monday evening, July 29, a rider had informed Colonel Cravens about the clash at Thomas Haley's place earlier in the day. Cravens sent for the Moderator company to assemble the next day. By noon on Tuesday about fifty Moderators had gathered and Cravens led a general discussion, with the conclusion "that the only alternative was to fight." The Regulators had miscalculated by arbitrarily ordering Sheriff Lewellyn, Jeff Cravens, Charles Lindsey, and other resolute leaders to abandon their land and homes. These prominent Moderators were the last men who would capitulate to tyrannical bullies with no legal authority, and they possessed the influence and leadership skills to rally other settlers to their side. "They mutually pledged themselves to kill every member of the committee should opportunity offer, and to stand by each other until the last Regulator was driven out of the country...." During the next few days other men rode into the Moderator camp, weapons at the ready.[18]

When Watt Moorman learned about the Moderator mustering, he began collecting more men and supplies, and he sent a detail to find a suitable location for fortification. Moorman had maintained contact with the large Regulator company in Harrison County, and now he dispatched a call for reinforcements. Undaunted by the prospect of battle, eighty to 100 Harrison County Regulators mustered as rapidly as possible, then began to march south toward Shelby County.[19]

Hilliard's ▲ Spring
Fortified by Regulators

Aug. 5　Moderators attack B'champ's
　　　　　One Moderator killed

　•　Regulators march to
　　　Hilliard's Spring

Church Hill Battle
　✳ Aug. 9

　•　Moderators follow to
　　　Church Hill

Aug. 9　Regulators attack
　　　　　Three Regulators killed

　•　Regulators march to
　　　Methodist Camp Ground

　•　Moderators camp below
　　　Shelbyville

N.

↑

Aug. 13　Regulators spring ambush
　　　　　No one killed

# SHELBY COUNTY
# BATTLEGROUND

August 1844

Beauchamp's
✳ Aug. 5
Fortified by Regulators

Shelbyville ■
　　　　　Ambush
　　　　✳ Aug. 13

Moderator ▲
Camp

MILES

1　2　3　4　5

Methodist Camp Ground

Fortified by ▲ Regulators

# 9 Battle

*"We all kept quiet until we got very*
*near then we gave the Texas yell as*
*no other people could yell."*
-- Eph Daggett

About three miles northwest of Shelbyville, on the property of Jerroboam Beauchamp, a dogtrot log cabin was under construction on a hill. A half-acre yard had been enclosed by a spilt-rail fence and "a large lot of lumber from the mills" had been hauled in to floor the cabin. Beauchamp's home was some distance away, and a Regulator patrol assigned to find a defensive site selected this hilltop location. Regulators stood the floor planks inside the fence, creating barricades which rifle balls could not penetrate. Colonel Watt Moorman brought his main body to this redoubt, then left to recruit reinforcements. By early August, the Regulators at Beauchamp's numbered sixty-two men, with many more – hopefully – on the way from Harrison County.[1]

Sixty-five Moderators assembled under Colonel Jeff Cravens. He sent a detachment of fifteen men to reconnoiter the Regulator position. Cravens instructed the scouts that if they encountered "any member of the proscribing committee to shoot them without warning." The home of Lewis Watkins, a member of the proscribing committee, stood along the path of the scouts, who were grimly eager to encounter this active Regulator. Alfred Truitt led the scouting party, which included Everett J. Ritter, who was on the proscribed list. Ritter had come from Tennessee to East Texas in 1831, when he was twenty-one, and by 1844 he was raising a large family on a

4,428-acre headright. His great-grandson, Tex Ritter, later gained fame as a Hollywood cowboy hero, but Everett engaged in real-life shooting adventures. Everett fought as a cavalryman during the Texas Revolution and as a Shelby County Moderator he was determined not to be driven from his land by Regulators.[3]

The Moderator party stopped at the Watkins cabin, but "much to their disappointment" they learned that he was absent. Assuming that he already had joined the Regulator camp, the scouts resumed their mission. But Watkins also was on the road, returning home from Shelbyville. Half a mile from his cabin, Watkins

encountered the Moderators. Although they let him pass, Everett Ritter suddenly threw his rifle to his shoulder and fired. The ball struck Watkins in the back of his neck and passed out near the jugular vein. He dropped from his horse and broke his arm in the fall. The Moderators rode on, thinking that Watkins was dead. But later he regained consciousness and rode home. Medical care saved his life, although Watkins suffered a permanent stiff neck.[4]

Grave marker of Jerroboam Beauchamp (1804-1858) in the Shelbyville Cemetery. Regulators forted up on Beauchamp's property in 1844, and after the ensuing battle employed his home as a Regulator hospital. *(Photo by the author)*

The Moderator scouting party arrived at the Regulator position. Most of the scouts concealed themselves and their horses in a timbered ravine while three men crept forward to find a vantage point. At a hill north of the Regulator redoubt, one scout climbed a tree and viewed the interior of the little fortification. After the party reunited, they rode into an open space about 200 yards in front of the Regulator position. There was a quick exchange of rifle fire, but the two factions were at maximum range and no one was hit. The scouts spurred away to report to Colonel Cravens. The Moderators decided "to attack the enemy's position with as little delay as possible."[5]

"I kept a sack of provisions and my horse close to my door," said Regulator Eph Daggett. Ready to join the fight at a moment's notice, he learned of the Regulator fortification at Beauchamp's farm. "I put on a clean shirt and clean summer pants and started for the rendezvous in five minutes. I got with six men and went to the battlegrounds a little before the Moderators came up."[6]

On Sunday night, August 4, the Regulators at Beauchamp's built a fire. With indications that a battle was imminent, the men were jumpy. When someone was heard approaching their position, Captain Joe Smith and John Farrar clambered on top of a log for a better look. One of them, probably Smith, lost his balance, and as he stumbled his gun discharged. The ball tore through Smith's hand and broke Farrar's arm; "thus was lost the services of two good men," grumped Regulator John Middleton.[7]

After spending a couple of days collecting ammunition, provisions, and a great many recruits, Colonel Cravens and the Moderators advanced toward the Regulator position. Planning an assault against a log cabin and a fence with plank breastworks, Cravens had tried without success to secure an artillery piece. The artillery piece that the Regulators had wheeled onto the courthouse square when Judge Ochiltree was in Shelbyville apparently had been taken to Matthew Brinson's blockhouse. The Moderators approached the Regulator redoubt on Monday morning, August 5. Outlying Regulator sentinels fired their rifles at long range, then hustled back into the redoubt.[8]

With their friends, neighbors, and relatives marching to battle, armed men swelled the ranks of the Moderators. John Middleton said there were 200 Moderators at Beauchamp's, while Eph Daggett thought there were 225 men under Cravens. Cravens sent a demand for surrender, which was ignored. Then Cravens divided his force into two companies. One Moderator contingent would attack the rear of the Regulator position, while Colonel Cravens would lead the balance of his men in a frontal assault.[9]

At mid-morning the Moderators advanced. Cravens "commenced a brisk fire in front which was warmly returned." But while the Regulators blazed away from the log cabin or from behind plank breastworks, Moderator riflemen were exposed in the open. Cravens ordered his men to pull back to the timber. Now both factions could fire from protected positions, but the range was too great to cause much damage.

A number of Moderators wanted to charge the redoubt, but others knew better than to advance across open ground against concealed riflemen. At the Battle of New Orleans in 1815, British regulars were shot to pieces by American riflemen behind cotton bales; afterward, British army instructions warned that frontal attacks against protected American riflemen would result in unacceptable costs. Texian riflemen, from the walls of the Alamo, had inflicted terrible punishment upon Mexican assault troops. Moderator Jonathan Anderson, a veteran of the Battle of San Jacinto, personally had witnessed advancing Texian riflemen shoot down Mexican

Three miles west of Shelbyville, this marker indicates the battleground where the Regulators and Moderators first fought in force in 1844. *(Photo by the author)*

soldiers by the hundreds. For every hotheaded Moderator who urged his comrades to charge, there were others who knew that an assault across open ground was foolhardy.

The long-range sniping match continued into the afternoon. While the Regulators were surrounded, a few Moderators rode into Shelbyville, only three miles to the southeast. Gunfire had been heard in town, and the Moderators bragged that Regulators "were being killed in heaps." Greatly alarmed, forty-four women who had husbands, brothers, sons, or sweethearts among the Regulators rode to the battlefield. They gathered and saddled mounts, then galloped in a group past the Moderators and on to the redoubt. "They looked wild," remarked Eph Daggett. The frantic women, expecting to see many dead loved ones, were relieved to find only a few wounded in the compound. After a brief visit, the women rode out, trading insults with the Moderators – who allowed them to pass in and out. Daggett heard one of the women shout at the Moderators, "You fight like cowards."[10]

The Regulators seemed to agree. "We became weary waiting for the charge," claimed Daggett. "One of our smart alecks got up on top of the fence, clapped his wings, crowed like a chicken and gobbled like a gobbler." Despite warnings from his comrades, this audacious character continued to cavort atop the fence. A Moderator marksman took aim at long range and carefully pressed the trigger. The ball inflicted a scalp wound and the man was knocked off the fence. "He was soon ready to fight again," reported Daggett, "but quit crowing and gobbling."[11]

Moderator sniper Bill Hansbury – perhaps the sharpshooter who shot the gobbler – was positioned in an oak tree. Hansbury targeted a Regulator who was firing from behind four-foot split boards that had been stacked three deep for a breastwork. During the day the sniper drove a dozen rifle balls into the boards, but each bullet passed through only the first or second plank, and the Regulator collected a pocketful of flattened slugs for remolding. Finally Hansbury exposed part of his body while he was reloading his rifle. The Regulator shot his nemesis out of the tree, and later the range was stepped off at an impressive 280 paces.[12]

It was an August day in East Texas, hot and humid, and by

afternoon men on both sides were desperate for water. There was a spring outside the redoubt, but no one from either side could approach it without falling under enemy fire from deadly range. Finally, late in the afternoon, Colonel Cravens ordered his men to withdraw to a creek about two miles distant. The Moderators camped beside the creek, and what became known as the First Battle came to a close.[13]

A great deal of powder and shot had been fired, but only a handful of men had been hit. Bill Hansbury was the only combatant killed on either side, while two other Moderators were wounded. Among the Regulator wounded, Jim Graham, shot through the mouth, was the most severely injured. "Eph M. Daggett had his pants cut, but was unhurt." The Regulators wounded were taken to Beauchamp's home and a physician named Davenport came out to tend the injuries.[14]

The Regulators pulled out of Beauchamp's after the fight during the night. The next day they linked up with Colonel Moorman and forty or fifty new Regulators. Now more than 100 strong, the Regulators headed for C.T. Hilliard's place, about fifteen miles northwest of Jerroboam Beauchamp's. At Hilliard's Spring near Flat Fork Creek, the Regulators felled a number of pine trees and fashioned a pen around the spring – inside this fortification there would be plenty of water. Many of the pine logs were split, and this crude planking was stacked against the pen to form protective barricades. The following day Colonel William T. Boulware and his Regulator company arrived from Harrison County, adding eighty to 100 men to the Shelby County force.[15]

During the fight at Beauchamp's, a Regulator courier sent for John Middleton, whose home was located fifteen miles north of Shelbyville and about eight miles east of Hilliard's. Middleton collected five neighboring Regulators, including Howell and Peter Hudson, and rode toward the battleground. Middleton's party was joined en route by two more men, enlarging the group to eight. Arriving after the battle and after the Regulators had moved north, Middleton and his men skirted the Moderator camp and rode toward Hilliard's.[16]

Other reinforcements arrived in small parties, swelling

Moorman's force to well over 200 men. Colonel Alexander Horton of San Augustine related that "enterprising young men from this county" ventured into Shelby County to enlist. "Usually their stay was short," observed Horton; "the cornbread and beef, the ticks, the heat, bad water, camp life and last but not least the crack of the deadly rifle was not to their liking." Horton pointed out that the Regulators and Moderators of Shelby County who were in the field campaigning were "in a state of unrest, thinking of their loved ones – their wives and children – left unprotected at home."[17]

Some of their wives, like their men, also were drawn to the martial adventure. "We had ladies out all the time acting as spies for us, watching the moderators," recalled John Middleton. He specifically mentioned Elizabeth White, wife of Captain Joe White; Mrs. M.T. Johnson, whose husband was a Regulator leader; Mrs. Nathan Matthews; and Helen Daggett Moorman. Helen's two brothers, Eph and Charles, were fighting with the Regulators, and despite a separation, she remained legally married to Colonel Watt Moorman. Helen eagerly rode through the woods, scouting Moderator movements. Like the forty-four women who passed back and forth through Moderator lines to visit their men at Beauchamp's, the female scouts relied upon their gender and Southern chivalry to keep them from becoming targets.[18]

The Moderators also had scouts. Colonel Cravens had sent out a "spy company" of twenty-five men. Cravens also sent men to recruit reinforcements and to procure ammunition and supplies. Within two days the Moderators received "a considerable number of recruits" from Shelby County, along "with a few from San Augustine and a small number from the State of Louisiana." Counting the scout company, Cravens commanded 165 men. "Perhaps there never was a more uncouth army (?) than this," described a participant. "Most of the men wore broad-brimmed wool hats, and jeans coats but in every conceivable style as suited the fancy of the wearer."[19]

The scout company returned to report the location and approximate size of the Regulator force. Cravens quickly readied his men, then set a line of march for Moorman's camp at Hilliard's

Spring. A log church which doubled as a school was located a couple of miles southwest of Hilliard's Spring, and Cravens planned to camp there on Church Hill before launching an attack on the Regulator position.

Cravens and the Moderators reached Church Hill about ten o'clock on Friday morning, August 9. The log church stood on a ridge between two streams, and Dave Strickland's home was nearby. Cravens directed his men to feed their horses and set up camp south of the church, and he posted sentinels. The Moderators stacked their rifles and began preparing a noon meal. Suddenly Helen Daggett Moorman boldly rode past the sentinels and into the camp. Asking for the commander, she was brought to Colonel Cravens. Helen launched a vehement but fictional complaint against some of his men. She claimed that while she was riding innocently nearby, a small party of Moderators had fired at her and she "had narrowly escaped with her life." Helen told Cravens that she believed him "to be an honorable and chivalrous gentleman, one who would not permit an unoffending and helpless woman to be put in peril...." She did not know the men, but expected him to discover and punish the culprits "for the honor of Texas." Cravens was "deeply mortified," and assured her that he would make every effort to discover their identity. Moderators clustered around to hear this exchange. While Helen's diatribe distracted the camp, the Regulators quietly moved into position to attack.[20]

Determined to play an active role in Shelby County's life-and-death-drama and not content with riding as a scout on the outskirts of the action, Helen Daggett Moorman had gone to Hilliard's Spring to talk with her estranged husband.[21] Colonel and Mrs. Moorman devised the ruse that facilitated a surprise attack by the Regulators. Colonel Moorman was unconcerned about the danger to his wife, while she was oblivious to the risk and eager for adventure. Excitedly Helen set out for the Moderator camp.

Colonel Moorman assigned M.T. Johnson to lead twenty-eight horsemen on a swing around the Moderator position so his cavalry company could attack from the south. The other Regulators marched overland. Colonel Boulware and Captain George Davidson led the Harrison County men and John Inman was in charge of the "Shelby Guards." Colonel Moorman, in overall command, planned to use his hunting horn to direct troop movement.[22]

The main body marched overland through the woods. Although the distance was only a couple of miles, it was another blazing hot August day and almost no one carried canteens. "We found a well and drew all the water out of it," recalled Eph Daggett. With 200 men crowding around a single well, the march was delayed. The Regulators were more than half a mile from the Moderator camp when they heard firing.[23]

Helen Moorman drew out her faux complaint to Colonel Cravens as long as possible, allowing the Regulators time to get into position. Finally departing, she had barely passed the last Moderator sentinel at noon when M.T. Johnson fired the first shot of the fight. His rifle ball struck the meat in a Moderator's hand. Immediately the other cavalrymen opened fire.[24]

"To arms! To arms!" The Moderators scrambled for their guns. Cooking and eating their midday meal, they were anticipating spending the afternoon in preparation for an assault the next day. Instead, suddenly and unexpectedly, they were under attack. Within moments they formed a hollow square and began returning fire. The Regulator cavalry company was badly outgunned and had no support from the main force, which still was tramping through the woods. "A general firing commenced and we ran pell-mell through it," said Eph Daggett. "They came up in a run, and were much heated and fatigued," remembered a Regulator cavalryman. Shouting "the Texas yell," the infantrymen burst into sight on the north and west sides of the church.[25]

A ravine offered a deadly vantage point just seventy-five yards from the rear of the Moderator camp. Colonel Cravens dispatched a detail to occupy the position that arrived just before Captain Davidson led a number of Harrison County Regulators onto the scene. There were no uniforms on either side, and Davidson mistakenly thought the Moderators were part of M.T. Johnson's men. Davidson called out to them and was answered by rifle and shotgun fire. Davidson was killed, Howell Hudson and a Harrison

County man named Kane were wounded fatally, and other Regulators were injured.[26]

Confusion between the two sides was widespread. "I was shot at twice by a Harrison County man by mistake," recorded Eph Daggett. Daggett and his brother Charles ran into Moderators in the woods. Recognizing Moderator Andy Truitt, they hurled him into a stream and escaped in the ensuing chaos. Daggett thought that Davidson, Hudson and Kane were shot "by our own men."[27]

A Harrison County Regulator named Dodd ran into the log church, which was supposed to have been seized by the cavalry company at the start of the fight. Inside, a wounded man begged for water. Dodd picked up a tin cup and outside found a spring within the Moderator perimeter. When he returned to the cabin, Dodd found several other Moderators inside whom he assumed were fellow Regulators. While he gave water to the wounded man, he chatted with the other combatants. Dodd's remarks aroused the suspicions of future Texas State Senator James Truitt, who asked to which company he belonged. "Col. Boulware's company from Harrison County," came the innocent reply. Truitt ordered Dodd taken prisoner, but told him he would be spared if he did not try to escape. Dodd was released several days later after the fighting subsided.[28]

As the combat intensified, William Nail led several other Moderators in a dash for the woods. These men, perhaps under fire for the first time in their lives, found safety deep in the forest and did not emerge until late the next morning.[29]

Eph Daggett, a courageous veteran of the blood feud, crept undetected to a ravine sheltering several Moderators and their horses. His shotgun misfired three times but on the fourth try finally blasted out a lethal pattern of buckshot. "A fine gray horse fell, a pony's leg was shot and one man got two balls in his thigh." Daggett added happily, "I never saw a creek bottom cleared so quickly. Just then four shots were fired at me from under the church and two were fired at me by my own men through mistake."[30]

With the Moderators firing from beneath and inside the log church, as well as other positions around the hill, the Regulators withdrew to the shelter of the woods. Like the Moderators did at

Beauchamp's a few days earlier, the Regulators opened up a determined fire against the defenders. But, again as at Beauchamp's, the range was too great for either side to be effective, while a charge up Church Hill would have been suicidal.

At midafternoon Colonel Moorman sounded three long blasts – the prearranged signal for withdrawal – on his hunting horn. M.T. Johnson led the cavalry out first to reoccupy the breastworks at Hilliard's Spring. The main force followed, but thinking there might be pursuit, John Middleton and a large contingent set an ambush. This band spent all night at the edge of the prairie near Church Hill, "and until 11 o'clock p.m. we continually heard groans and lamentations," recalled Middleton. During the night, Colonel Cravens pulled the Moderators off Church Hill and moved back four miles as a precaution.[31]

The next morning Eph Daggett and other Regulators, finding Church Hill deserted, went forward to inspect the log building. "There was blood, hair and even teeth everywhere." The church had served as the Moderator hospital, and at least one man had been shot in the mouth. The Regulators assumed that casualties had been heavy. Middleton stated that "sixteen were acknowledged killed and twenty-five were known to have been wounded." Such numbers were exaggerated. Dr. Ashcroft testified that "the Moderators had none killed and but six wounded, all of whom recovered." In addition to three dead, the Regulators suffered a dozen wounded. Davidson, Hudson, and Kane were buried near Hilliard's Spring.[32]

Regulators called the clash the Battle of Church Hill. But since the Regulators had suffered three fatalities and they apparently had "retired in considerable disorder," Moderators proudly named the battle "Helen's Defeat."[33]

On the morning after Helen's Defeat, Colonel Cravens sent scouts to reconnoiter the Regulator camp. Probing carefully, by the time the scouts reached Hilliard's Spring the Regulators were gone. Cravens and most of his men believed that the Regulators had retreated north to Harrison County. Cravens decided to march to Shelbyville and camp at the Methodist Camp Ground several miles south of town where he would replenish his ammunition and supplies before resuming hostilities. As the force proceeded south, two female Moderator scouts intercepted the march. These valiant women informed Cravens that the Regulators had moved south, not north, and already had occupied the Methodist Camp Ground.[34]

Cravens decided to camp in a field a mile or so south of Shelbyville and a few miles north of the Regulator camp. A "dark-looking log" was placed on a set of wagon wheels, and this *faux* "cannon" occupied a conspicuous position in front of the Moderator camp. While Cravens planned his next attack, a number of Moderators decided they had had enough fighting and slipped away to their homes. Counting a few new recruits, Cravens still had about 150 men under arms. The district attorney of San Augustine County, future governor Oran M. Roberts, remarked upon how large bodies of men could sustain themselves in the East Texas countryside. Roberts pointed out "that the woods abounded with fat cattle and hogs, and their wives and boys and old men carried them cornmeal and bread, both day and night, selecting routes that would evade interception by the enemy." In addition to this informal logistics

The Last Battle monument is located just south of Shelbyville, where the final skirmishing between Regulators and Moderators took place on August 14, 1844. *(Photo by the author)*

system, Dr. Ashcroft related that a few "men of wealth" supported the Regulator cause. These prosperous sponsors were "abundantly able to furnish them with everything they might require."[35]

The Regulators fortified the Methodist Camp Ground with log breastworks while Moderator scouts observed their position. Apparently aware of such scouting patrols, Colonel Moorman planned an ambush for Tuesday morning, August 13. Moorman would lead a fifteen-man detachment concealed on the San Augustine Road, heading south out of Shelbyville; Colonel Boulware and a similar detail were positioned on the Natchitoches Road, which angled southeast off the San Augustine Road; and George Standford set an ambush along the Sand Hills Road, angling westward. These men concealed themselves on foot; their horses were left tied at the head of a hollow about half a mile from Moorman's position.[36]

At daybreak, half a dozen Moderators led by Richard Haley rode unsuspectingly toward Moorman's location. Moorman, hidden with his men in a thick stand of pine trees on the east side of the road, had directed that he would fire the first shot. Waiting until the Moderators were only twenty yards away, Moorman squeezed his trigger. The gun misfired, but the next man triggered a shot. This ball struck the lock of Richard Haley's rifle, causing it to discharge. The other Regulators opened fire, but only Mark Haley was wounded. Haley was struck by a ball which passed through his leg and penetrated his horse. The startled Moderators spurred their mounts and headed into the woods on the opposite side of the road, riding back toward their nearby camp.[37]

Mark Haley's wounded horse collapsed, but he scrambled into the woods. The five Moderators who remained mounted faced another volley of gunfire from Standford's men. No one was wounded, and the Moderators skirted Standford's position and galloped west toward camp, where the gunfire had been heard. The five horsemen reached the Moderator position within a few minutes. Mark Haley, despite his leg wound, hiked into camp later in the morning.[38]

Back at the ambush site, the Regulators reassembled and retrieved their horses. Colonel Boulware picked up a Moderator hat from the road. Since the Moderators had vanished, the Regulators rode south to their camp. Moorman brandished the captured hat and bragged that four Moderators had been killed, but his men soon learned that all of the ambush victims had escaped. One respected Regulator mused "that if fifteen men in ambush could not bring even one man to the ground out of a party of six..., the cause must be inhumanly bad." Only four days earlier the Regulators had been repulsed at Church Hill; now their commander had failed to execute an ambush "with every advantage." Regulator recruits who "had been promised liberal wages, but as yet had received nothing but rough fare," became discouraged and began to leave camp.[39]

Franklin Farrar had joined the Regulators because several other family members already had enlisted with Moorman. John Farrar, Franklin's brother, had an arm broken by a bullet at Beauchamp's, and Franklin asked for leave to visit his injured sibling. Colonel Moorman refused, stating "that a decisive battle was daily expected and every man must be at his post prepared to perform his duty." Franklin Farrar typified the individualistic frontiersmen who volunteered for military service, and such men had to be handled with tact by their commanders. Moorman's authoritative manner incensed Farrar, who unleashed a stream of oaths at the colonel. Ignoring Moorman's threats to arrest him, Farrar shouldered his rifle and angrily stalked out of camp. Colonel Moorman sensibly did not order his arrest.[40]

Anxious to lift Regulator morale with a successful move, Moorman dispatched John Middleton to the home of John Choate, where two wounded Moderators had been taken. The injured Moderators, Whetstone and Castleberry -- a son of Peter Whetstone from Marshall and a brother of two Regulators, Stephen and Aaron Castleberry -- were casualties of the Battle of Church Hill. Word arrived at the Choate cabin of the approach of a Regulator posse. Castleberry, who had recovered part of his strength, ran into an orchard behind the cabin just as the Regulators rode up. They shot at him, but Castleberry disappeared unscathed into the forest. Meanwhile, women in the house had concealed the seriously injured

Whetstone under the floor. The Regulators searched indoors and outside for Whetstone, but Middleton finally led his men back toward camp.[41]

With the Moderators resupplied and confident after Helen's Defeat, Colonel Cravens decided to attack the Regulator camp. "His men were in high spirits and greatly elated by their recent success," reported Dr. Ashcroft. "Some of them actually believed that they could not be slain by a Regulator, and asserted that they were especially protected by Providence."[42]

Wary of another Regulator ambush, Cravens ordered his men off the road, where they struggled through the woods in a southerly direction. Progress was slowed badly, and when the Moderators reached a creek with steep banks, Cravens decided to camp for the night. The creek banks were eight to ten feet deep, a natural fortification in case of attack. The Regulator camp was only a mile and a half away, and Cravens sent out his scouting company to gain information prior to an attack the next day.

But Regulator sentinels had spotted the Moderator scouts, and Colonel Moorman leaped at the opportunity to attack the enemy while twenty-five of their men were absent from camp. Moorman mustered his entire force and headed north, although the location of the Moderators was unknown. After marching a mile or so, the Regulators encountered a Moderator sympathizer named Bowles who was returning from a mill. Questioned about the location of the Moderator camp, the feisty old man retorted that if he attacked the Moderators, Moorman would have the pleasure of supping that night with his friend and patron, the Devil. Moorman pressed Bowles for an answer, and he replied that the camp was "down that creek there a few hundred yards."

Moorman asked how many Moderators were in camp. "About one hundred," said Bowles, "the rest are out on scout."

"If you deceive me," growled Moorman, "I'll hang you to the first limb I come to after I make the discovery, you old rogue."

"If you'll hang all the rogues in your own camp first, you'll have no ropes to spare," snapped Bowles, adding an oath.

A council of war then took place between Colonel Moorman

and Colonel Boulware. Moorman wanted Boulware and his Harrison County men to lead the attack, insisting "that he was too well known to venture within gunshot of the enemy." Boulware scoffed. He had led the assault on Church Hill and his division had suffered severe casualties. Besides, it was Moorman's duty, since the Harrison County men comprised "an auxiliary and had no personal interest in the matter."

Bowles overheard the argument and stepped forward to express his sarcastic regret that they could not agree. "I will suggest a plan that will probably remove that difficulty," he said with sly malice. "Just march down this hill in the direction of the creek about two hundred yards further and I'll be d—d if the engagement don't bring itself on."

Moorman was thrown "into a perfect fury of rage," again threatening Bowles. The dispute between Moorman and Boulware became inflamed, and Boulware threatened to take his men back to Harrison County. The two colonels finally cooled down, then inconclusively pulled their men back to their fortified camp to await a Moderator attack.

That evening the Moderator scouting company rode back into camp and reported that Moorman, Boulware, and nearby twenty other Regulator leaders took breakfast at a house half a mile from the camp. Cravens began to formulate a plan to launch an early morning attack that would cut off the breakfasting officers from their men. Before this plan could be carried out, however, a courier galloped into camp with a proclamation from President Sam Houston.[43]

Eph Daggett and a party of Regulators were probing a canebrake which they thought sheltered a number of the enemy. A young woman galloped into their midst and asked the whereabouts of several men who were Moderators. The surprised reply was an indication toward the canebrake. "I want them to get away," she explained excitedly. "Sam Houston's militia is on their way to Shelby on the Shelby Road."[44]

She rode away looking for her relatives. Recognizing several Regulators, she cried out in alarm: "My God."

Men crowded around her, and one Regulator pointed his gun at her. When she refused to answer their questions, she was accused of being a spy. The gunman told her that "it was the rules of war to kill all spies when caught in the enemies' camp, and this was most certainly war." Ominously he cocked his gun.

"I am no spy," she insisted. "I only came hunting my husband and brother to tell them Sam Houston had a big army of men not three miles from here."

Watt Moorman overheard the exchange and made a decision. He brought his hunting horn to his lips and sounded three blasts.

Sam Houston during his second presidency, when he came to San Augustine to halt the Regulator-Moderator War. *(Courtesy East Texas Research Center, Stephen F. Austin State University, Nacogdoches)*

# 10 Houston and the Militia

*"Be it resolved that we do hereby forever discard the odious designations of the Regulator and Moderator, and will henceforth be hailed and recognized by no other name than that of Texans."*
--Truce document

At dawn on September 21, 1826, Tennessee Congressman Sam Houston and General William A. White took their positions at a dueling ground just across the state line in Kentucky. General White had challenged Houston, who chose pistols at fifteen feet. At the signal Houston shot White through the groin. Although it was thought that White would die, he recovered after a four month convalescence.

Six years later Houston was criticized in print because of an action taken while he was governor of Tennessee. He initiated a challenge to his critic, Ohio Congressman William Stanbery, who simply ignored Houston. Soon afterward the men encountered each other on the streets of Washington. Although Stanbery pulled a pistol, Houston delivered a vicious caning with his hickory walking stick.

In 1814, at the Battle of Horseshoe Bend, Lieutenant Houston fought with conspicuous valor until he collapsed from wounds. In 1836 General Houston's ankle was shattered by a Mexican bullet while he led the Texian army to a spectacular victory at San Jacinto.

Raised in Virginia and the backwoods of Tennessee, Houston

was a Southerner and a frontiersman, touchy about his honor and courageous in combat. He understood the Southern frontiersmen who engaged in the Regulator-Moderator conflict of East Texas and he seemed inclined to let them fight it out as long as the disturbance was confined to a limited area. When the first two Regulators were killed in Harrison County in 1840, Houston, having completed his first term as president of the Republic of Texas, practiced law in Nacogdoches and San Augustine and served as a congressman from Nacogdoches. In 1841, while the conflict heated up and spread to Shelby County, Houston won his second term as president and was inaugurated in December.

In 1842, the first full year of President Houston's second administration, Senator Robert Potter was killed by Regulators in Harrison County. The death of Potter, a chronic troublemaker and a bitter political enemy, could not have surprised or bothered Houston greatly. Otherwise, only a handful of East Texas ruffians died in a few incidents in 1842. During this year Houston had to deal with two brief but troubling invasions by Mexican forces. He also reopened annexation negotiations with the United States and pursued stringent measures to reduce government expenses. One key reduction involved limiting the Texas military to a few Ranger companies and unpaid militia units in various counties. President Houston had scant military power to employ in East Texas and more pressing matters elsewhere demanded his attention. Furthermore, there were only three Regulator-Moderator fatalities the next year, in 1843. During the first two years of his three-year term -- December 1841 to December 1844 -- Houston ignored the Regulator-Moderator conflict to concentrate on larger events.

Then, early in 1844, Judge John Hansford was murdered in Harrison County by a posse of Regulators. Violence rapidly escalated in Shelby County, and by summer the two factions were clashing with large bodies of armed men. With surprising speed, news of each fight was "carried to all the surrounding country in Eastern Texas, which caused many persons in the adjacent counties to have strong feelings in favor of one or the other side; so that there was really danger of the spirit of hostile antagonism spreading beyond the limits of Shelby County." This observation was made by San

Augustine District Attorney Oran M. Roberts, who was aware that this "spirit of hostile antagonism" also had wracked Harrison County. "This feeling was becoming very strong in San Augustine County, which caused Judge William A. Ochiltree and many prominent citizens residing there to interest themselves to have this war stopped." Judge Ochiltree, Roberts, and others wrote to President Houston in Washington-on-the-Brazos, requesting him "to come to San Augustine to take steps to have the combatants lay down their arms." Houston had ignored a petition from San Augustine in 1841, and in the summer of 1844 he again "seemed very tardy about coming...."[1]

The great man did come, finally, in mid-August. Likely Houston had heard rumors of Watt Moorman's plans to lead a revolution – Dr. Levi Ashcroft stated that the substance of the meeting on July 28 of Moorman's Provisional Committee "was soon made known in the most remote portions of the county...." President Houston at last responded to the entreaties of old friends in San Augustine, traveling from Washington-on-the-Brazos to Nacogdoches, where he enlisted a former comrade-in-arms, General Thomas J. Rusk. As secretary of war, Rusk had fought bravely alongside Houston at San Jacinto. Elected to represent Nacogdoches in the Second Congress of the Republic, Rusk was selected to chair the House Military Committee. In that capacity he sponsored the Militia Bill, and twice

Thomas J. Rusk conducted a successful defense for the men who killed Robert Potter and later helped President Houston put down the Regulator-Moderator War. *(Courtesy East Texas Research Center, Stephen F. Austin State University, Nacogdoches)*

Rusk served as major general of militia. Riding together from Nacogdoches to San Augustine, Rusk and Houston discussed a plan of action along the way.[2]

Arriving in San Augustine on Friday, August 16, Houston established presidential headquarters at the Mansion House, a two-story, frame hotel with a large gallery across the front. There Houston greeted Judge William Ochiltree, District Attorney Oran M. Roberts, Colonel Travis Broocks, and several other trusted men from the area. Houston led the way to a woodpile out back where the group whittled and discussed the situation. Plans were formulated, messages dispatched, and correspondence drafted. Late that evening Roberts rode back by the hotel and "saw two very large men – Houston and Rusk – arm in arm, promenading in that long piazza, with beaming faces and cheerful talk, in mellow mood, indicating that they had undergone a spirited communion after the council of war."[3]

Couriers rode into Shelby County with a predated presidential proclamation:

> Executive Department, San Augustine,
> August 15th, 1844.
>
> It having been represented to me that there exists in the county of Shelby a state of anarchy and misrule – that parties are arrayed against each other in hostile attitude, contrary to law and order. –
>
> Now therefore, Be it known, that I, Sam Houston, President of the Republic of Texas, to the end that hostilities may cease and good order prevail, command all citizens engaged therein to lay down their arms and retire to their respective homes.
>
> Given under my hand and seal this day and year above written,
>
> *Sam Houston*[4]

A courier reached Colonel Jeff Cravens while he was planning a dawn attack against the Regulator camp. Cravens immediately abandoned his plans, "hoping that good order and quiet might yet be restored" by President Houston without further bloodshed. "In truth, all parties were glad of the turn events had taken," stated Dr. Ashcroft. "They had nothing to gain by continuance of the struggle and many of them much to lose." Colonel Alexander Horton, who marched in with the first company sent by Houston, noted the same relieved attitude: "All parties in Shelby hailed the militia with joy as a sure way out of their troubles."[5]

When Colonel Watt Moorman learned of the presence of President Houston and that militia units had been dispatched, dreams of revolution vanished. "Watt gave a few blasts on his horn" to summon his men, related Regulator Eph Daggett. "We will have to disband for a while," announced Moorman, who described the approach of "several companies" of militia. "Every man take the open course and take the best care of himself."[6]

"Such a stampede I never saw before," reported an amused Daggett. "The pine knots flew ten feet high, knocked by the horses' feet as the rowels entered their sides. The woods were the nearest way home. Some did not go home for a long time, and some left the country, I for one." John Middleton and several others fled across the international border into Louisiana. Colonel William Boulware led his company back toward Harrison County. Watt Moorman, accompanied by as many as thirty loyal riders, went north to the redoubt recently constructed at Hilliard's Spring.[7]

President Houston followed his initial, brief proclamation with a longer "Letter to My Countrymen." Houston emphasized that it was his duty "to suppress all insurrectionary movements," and he announced his intention to use the militia to restore order. He pointed out that he had not yet had time to evaluate the total situation, and that he would take "a mild and advisory course" in dealing with conditions in Shelby County:

San Augustine, August 16, 1844

My Countrymen: It has been communicated to me from various sources, that much excitement has existed amongst the citizens of Shelby, and that they are generally arrayed under different leaders, in opposition to each other, and to the great terror and alarm of peaceful inhabitants. Such acts and doings are contrary to the constitution and laws of the country. I have been invested with power and authority, as Chief Magistrate, to suppress all insurrectionary movements, and to that end the militia of the country have been placed subject to my orders. All those concerned, must be aware of the deleterious influence that such associations will have upon our national character abroad, as well as the destructive influence which such acts must have upon our social and political institutions, where disorders of such character exist. All classes and conditions of life must feel insecure in their personal safety and property. If persons in society have rendered themselves obnoxious to the laws, it remains with the laws to punish them -- but not for individuals to place themselves above the law, and assume authority to themselves powers which belong to the constituted authorities of the country alone.

It has not been in my power to possess myself with all the causes which led to this condition of things. Therefore, I abstain from making decisions as to the merits or demerits of the parties. At the same time I feel it to be my duty, for the discharge of which I am responsible to my country, to admonish those who are now arrayed against each other, in violation of the peace of the community, to disperse and return to their respective homes, and to abstain from all acts of violence toward those who are under the protection of the laws. This is a mild

and advisory course; and I trust will be regarded in
such manner as will render it unnecessary to have
recourse to such measures as would be as unpleasant
to myself as they would be indispensable to arrest
the unhappy conditions of things, which I am
informed now exits in Shelby County.

*Sam Houston*[8]

During his first week in San Augustine, August 16 – 23,
President Houston sent a stream of correspondence to the colonels
of militia in San Augustine, Nacogdoches, and Sabine counties, and
to Brigadier General James Smith, whose plantation was in the center
of what became Rusk County. Houston directed the three colonels
and their various companies to serve as a "brigade" under General
Smith. At fifty-two, James Smith was six months older than Sam
Houston, and like Houston he had served under General Andrew
Jackson during the War of 1812. Smith came to Texas from Tennessee
in 1834, and when the Texas Revolution broke out, he returned to
Tennessee to organize a company of volunteers. During the Cherokee
War of 1839 Smith again raised a company. This able warrior was a
personal friend to both Sam Houston and Thomas J. Rusk, as well
as future governor J. Pinckney Henderson. When Rusk County was
organized, Smith donated land for a county seat, stipulating that
the town be named "Henderson".[9]

President Houston wrote at least three letters to Colonel
Travis G. Broocks, a prominent citizen of San Augustine who
commanded the county militia. Colonel Broocks could have received
oral instructions, but the president wanted him to hold official
authorization on paper. Broocks received two brief communications
on Monday, August 19, including one that went to all three colonels:

San Augustine, August 19, 1844.

To Colonels T.G. Broocks, San Augustine; W.M.
Means, Sabine; John Todd, Nacogdoches:
Sirs, -- You will immediately take the proper steps
to have your command in readiness for marching

orders, armed and equipped for any emergency. You will consider this order sufficient, after any notification from authority, and act as it may command.

*Sam Houston*

The other note received on Monday by Colonel Broocks ordered him to take immediate action. "You will forthwith proceed to the scene of contest in Shelby County, and enforce the laws of the country, with the force under your command. Order must and shall be restored in the county...." During the few days since Houston's arrival, a sizeable company had gathered in San Augustine. Large numbers of men were soon expected from other counties, but

Colonel Alexander "Sandy" Horton of San Augustine years after his involvement in the Regulator-Moderator War. *(Courtesy John and Betty Oglesbee of San Augustine)*

the president decided that Broocks and the San Augustine men could make an initial show of force. Broocks would be accompanied by Colonel Alexander Horton, acting in the capacity of marshal of Texas.

Colonel Broocks and about eighty mounted men rode twenty miles to Shelbyville and pitched their tents just south of town and within view of the Moderator camp. Presumably Colonel Broocks and Marshal Horton held discussions with Colonel Cravens during the evening. The next morning, seemingly by prearrangement, Broocks demanded a surrender in the name of

President Houston. "Cravens immediately ordered his men to lay down their arms, and submit themselves to the order," related Moderator surgeon Levi Ashcroft. "The men cheerfully obeyed the command and the marshal produced the writ and proceeded to arrest ten of the leading men," including Colonel Cravens and Sheriff Lewellyn.

Marshal Horton and an escort rode with these ten Moderator leaders toward San Augustine. The other Moderators were instructed to remain in camp "until further orders from the proper authorities," while Colonel Broocks marched to the Regulator camp, which had been abandoned.[10]

Other militiamen continued to reach San Augustine by the hundreds. The call to arms had been issued by Sam Houston, victor of San Jacinto. Houston, a larger-than-life man of legendary accomplishments, was enormously admired. He had been a combat hero at twenty-one, a U.S. congressman, major general of Tennessee militia, governor of Tennessee, protégé of Andrew Jackson, general of the Texian army, the first elected president of the Republic of Texas, and the only man to twice win election as president. A politician of surpassing skill and ambition, Houston later served the state of Texas as U.S. senator and governor. Although reviled by numerous political enemies, Houston commanded deep respect and popularity among the great majority of Texans.

When this man of almost mythical reputation and towering achievements called for volunteers, his fellow Texans surged to his summons. Some – perhaps many – had served under him in 1836; others, too young eight years earlier, now had their opportunity. Some volunteers probably had never drilled with a militia unit. The county militia companies were informal and unfunded; members provided their own guns, ammunition, supplies, horses, and horse feed.

Colonel Broocks repeatedly asked if the Republic could furnish provisons for his men and horses, or if ordnance might be procured from the U.S. Army at Fort Jesup. President Houston's reply was almost apologetic over the lack of available resources, and he insisted that the militia should not worsen conditions in Shelby County:

San Augustine, 23rd August, 1844

To Colonel T.G. Broock[s]:

Sir, -- I have the honor to acknowledge your dispatches of the 20th and 23rd instant. After noting their contents, I have to remark, that it would not be possible to obtain either ordnance or any other supplies from Fort Jesup. The regulations of the United States army inhibit any officer to loan or dispose of any public arms, or stores, on pain of being dismissed from the service.

As relates to the subject of supplies for the army now in camp, I can only assure you Congress made no appropriation for such service, and I dare make no expenditure not sanctioned by law. Considering the scarcity of corn for the inhabitants of Shelby County, the horses should be grazed on grass, but not fed with corn – or it may greatly distress the community.

I have written to Gen. Smith, to whom you are referred, as I am greatly pressed for time.

*Sam Houston*

More than 500 men eventually assembled in San Augustine. They were organized into a brigade by General Smith and by their colonels, and this formidable column marched into Shelby County. General Smith linked up with Colonel Broocks at the deserted Regulator camp, producing a combined force of 600 fighting men. This army, expertly led by combat veterans, dwarfed any force the Regulators or Moderators could hope to put in the field. President Houston intended to stage a martial demonstration that would intimidate the warring factions and halt the violence and any revolutionary plans.

With Colonel Cravens and other Moderator leaders in custody, a search was launched for Watt Moorman and prominent Regulators. Colonel Broocks rode with his men to Hilliard's Spring, while another company went to the home of John Middleton.

Middleton and other Regulators had retreated ahead of the militia army into Louisiana. But word reached them that Howell Hudson – whose home was located northeast of Middleton's – had died of wounds received at the Battle of Church Hill, and they returned to Texas to aid in the burial of their comrade. "We buried him with military honors," said Middleton, "firing a platoon over his grave."[11]

Observing what they thought was a "spy of the moderators" -- the rider may have been a militia scout -- the burial party "chased him five miles but he escaped." Then they encountered Watt Moorman, who brought them drinks of "Bust-head" at a nearby grog shop. After departing, Middleton and his friends crossed paths with Moorman's father and another man: "they told us to turn back that the militia were at Hilliard's and eighty men were coming in our direction." The party backtracked, but when they passed the grog shop, nine men again stopped – "they wanted more liquor."

Middleton learned that a militia company had searched his home and confiscated provisions. His party sighted another militia group with Watt Moorman in custody, but "we turned and made our escape." Pushing eastward, that night they again left Texas and crossed the Sabine River.

Watt Moorman had been arrested by an advance guard of Colonel Broocks' San Augustine company. Marshal Horton had returned immediately to Shelby County after delivering the Moderator leaders to San Augustine, and he was one of the half-dozen men who captured Moorman. Moorman had just treated a number of Regulators to drinks, after drinking heavily himself since the previous night. Returning to Hilliard's Spring from the grog shop, he saw the militia party and drunkenly thought they were some of his men. Moorman rode into their midst and found himself facing an array of firearms. "Hand over your gun to Col. Horton," he was ordered. Reluctantly Moorman complied, then was told to hand over his pistols. Although he denied having any, the proximity of a double-barreled shotgun persuaded him to give two handguns to Horton. Finally he was forced to surrender a bowie knife.[12]

Moorman tried to blow his hunting horn to alert his men, but "he was politely informed that he had, in all probability, blown his last blast." At this point John Middleton and his party rode up, then rapidly galloped away. When Colonel Broocks reached his advance guard with their prisoner, he decided to return to Shelbyville. At nightfall Broocks established camp at the farm of Dave Strickland. Moorman was taken into a cornfield and ringed by a thirty-man guard. He was provided with blankets, but he spent the night pacing nervously and muttering to himself. Reaching Shelbyville the next day, they learned that Matthew Brinson, M.T. Johnson, Eph Daggett, and six other prominent Regulators had surrendered and had been sent under guard to San Augustine. Watt Moorman was the tenth Regulator taken into custody, and ten Moderators already had been brought to San Augustine.[13]

Watt Moorman thought that Alexander "Sandy" Horton wanted to kill him. "Watt promised him a killing some time in the future," related Eph Daggett, who remarked upon Moorman's lack of "prudence." But Horton was surprised at the impression made by his prisoner. "Morman [sic] had nothing of the appearance of a desperado – courteous, affable and gentlemanly. In appearance he was a fine looking specimen of the genus homo, with a rather military air as if born to command."[14]

General Smith and President Houston kept a team of couriers racing back and forth between the army and San Augustine. General Smith intended to keep the president informed of his movements, of the arrests, and of "negotiations" with the captives. On Friday, August 23, President Houston expressed his gratitude, along with his conviction that "the appearance of the military was necessary to suppress the insurrectionary movements which had for some time existed in Shelby County." Emphasizing the importance of maintaining "the majesty of the constitution and the laws," he suggested that a company be left in Shelbyville "subject to the orders of the Honorable W.B. Ochiltree," who also sent instructions. Conscious of expenses, President Houston urged "that the greatest care and economy should be used in sustaining the troops," and that the army soon would be discharged. "You will be careful to secure all who surrender, their persons and property inviolate from any indignity."[15]

Couriers must have met each other on the road, because that same afternoon General Smith sent a note which reached

Houston that night at nine o'clock. The president wrote an immediate reply. Three days later, with order restored, Houston instructed General Smith to leave in Shelbyville "a company of mounted men, to consist of at least fifty-six rank and file," who would be led by a captain and two lieutenants. The company would be stationed in Shelbyville for three months. The rest of the army was discharged, following a final night in camp outside Shelbyville. But in case of further "insurrectionary purposes," General Smith was to raise another force and, if necessary, "proclaim martial law ... as the emergency may demand."[16]

Colonel Leonard Mabbitt of San Augustine agreed to remain camped at Shelbyville with a militia company. Although the men under his command totaled only about half the number suggested by Houston, the presence of thirty armed cavalrymen was a daily reminder of the power that could be exercised by the Republic of Texas. It was understood that Mabbitt's company was in Shelbyville "to keep the peace and assist the civil officers if it became necessary." The militia company remained quartered at Shelbyville until late December 1844, a deployment of four months instead of three. The San Augustine militia members found month after month of guard duty to be boring and personally unprofitable, and Captain Mabbitt had to issue an appeal for volunteers to keep his ranks filled.[17]

After the Regulator and Moderator leaders arrived in San Augustine, they were confined in the courthouse. "The court house was quite full of the Shelby prisoners," described Sandy Horton, "in from their camp life without changing their clothes." These disheveled prisoners were addressed by President Houston, who intended to extend leniency after impressing upon them the force of his personality and authority. "Houston, in the zenith of his glory, appeared before them," related Horton; "he talked to them as a loving father would talk to a lot of bad boys who had been quarreling among themselves." Judge Ochiltree assigned bail "in heavy sums," which they provided. Then, pointedly, "they were told to go in peace."[18]

Immediately upon his release, Watt Moorman was arrested by the sheriff of San Augustine County for the murder of John N.

Bradley. Moorman was taken before a justice of the peace who conducted a brief examination, then bound him over for trial. "Heavy irons were put upon his feet and hands," related Dr. Ashcroft with undisguised satisfaction, "and he was confined in the dungeon of the county jail."[19]

Bail was set so high that it was assumed Moorman would remain in confinement. But there were well-to-do men who had supported the Regulator cause and now acted as his sureties. Upon his release, Moorman returned to Shelbyville, where he was struck by the change of attitude toward him. No longer was he "courted and flattered and feared by everyone," according to Dr. Ashcroft. Respectable men "now met him with cold formality that plainly indicated their desire to cur his acquaintance." Rural citizens "who had once feared to visit Shelbyville without his permission now passed him in the street without notice." Tried within a few weeks of his arrest, Moorman was acquitted on the grounds that John Bradley had threatened his life – a solid defense in Texas, as well as in other Western states and territories, throughout the nineteenth century. Moorman left East Texas for a time. When he returned to Shelby County he maintained "a precarious existence" as a gambler. Watt and Helen Moorman had a daughter in 1845, but they were afraid to leave home after dark for fear of ambush by Moderators. The couple later divorced.[20]

Judge William B. Ochiltree returned to Shelbyville early in October 1844 for the fall term of district court. No one was to be "seriously prosecuted for acts done during the Shelby war," reported Sandy Horton, but a considerable backlog of trial work had accumulated. "The court was attended by almost every man in the county," remembered Dr. Ashcroft. The militia company was still on duty in Shelbyville at that point, and "was kept in constant readiness to suppress any riot or disturbance."[21]

All went smoothly on Monday and Tuesday, October 7 and 8. But at the close of court on Tuesday afternoon, as Alfred Truitt mounted his horse, he saw Charles A. Luton shouldering his way through the crowd while brandishing a double-barreled shotgun. Truitt threw himself off his mount just as Luton fired, but the blast sailed harmlessly above the horse. Pulling a pistol, Truitt fired from beneath his horse's neck. The heavy ball fractured Luton's shoulder and ended the fight. The militia company immediately surrounded the crowd and Truitt surrendered to custody. Although the trouble "was something connected with the late disturbances," Truitt was tried and acquitted on grounds of self-defense. Luton had to put up bail during his convalescence, "but forfeited his bond by leaving the country for parts unknown."[22]

The decisive response of the militia company impressed the public, and there were no more incidents during the court term. Judge Ochiltree commanded great respect, and while still on the bench in Shelbyville he determined to use his position to try to bring an official end to the Regulator-Moderator hostilities. He called in five other respected men: D.S. Kaufman, attorney and political leader, and Amos Clark of Nacogdoches County; B.G. Burke and W.H. Landrum of Sabine County; and Isaac Van Zandt of Harrison County. Judge Ochiltree chaired this delegation of prominent citizens who had played no role in the Regulator-Moderator War. Their deliberations resulted in a document drafted by Kaufman:[23]

We, the undersigned citizens of the Republic of Texas, in view of the disastrous consequences – the anarchy and misrule attendant upon the late attempt in the county of Shelby and elsewhere to turn the law from its legitimate channels, and to the end that law and order may prevail, peace and quietude be restored, do hereby solemnly pledge ourselves to assist the civil authorities in carrying out, maintaining and enforcing the law of the country. And to that end,

1st. Be it resolved that we do hereby forever discard the odious designations of Regulator and Moderator, and will henceforth be hailed and recognized by no other name than that of Texans.

2nd. Resolved that we will forget and forgive, and will frown upon and discountenance any and every attempt to revive the unfortunate divisions that have so long distracted our country. That we will give the hand of fellowship to every worthy citizen, no matter under which party banner he may have rallied.

3rd. Resolved that a voice has come to us from our firesides, from our wives and little ones; that its pleadings for peace shall not pass unheeded and we do hereby pledge our sacred honor to the strict observance and faithful performance of the foregoing resolutions.

*James Truitt*
*John Dial*
*M. T. Johnson*
*John H. McNairy*

Judge Ochiltree and his delegation persuaded four influential Shelby County men to sign the document before it was circulated among the public. Truitt and Dial were Moderators who recently had won election to the Texas Congress over Regulators Johnson and McNairy. With these four quality signatures, the document was printed and distributed throughout the county. A great many men signed the document, including citizens who had taken no part in the conflict. Judge Ochiltree returned to San Augustine with a hopeful sense of accomplishment. "The 'Regulators' and 'Moderators,' as organized bodies, ceased to exist," proclaimed Oran M. Roberts, "and

In a long and distinguished career, Oran M. Roberts served as governor of Texas, chief justice of the Texas Supreme Court, professor of law at the University of Texas – and San Augustine's district attorney in 1844. More than half a century later, Roberts wrote, "from memory, without notes or memoranda," a first-person account of "The Shelby War" for *The Texas Magazine.* (Internet photo)

the `Shelby War'... was ended."[24]

The war was ended, but not the hard feelings that had been generated by four years of violence. A few days after the district court session ended, a fatal clash exploded in Shelbyville between Moderator Vardeman Duncan and Regulator Albert Harris. Harris had mounted his horse to leave town, but Duncan angrily hit him with a stick and dragged him out of the saddle. Duncan drew a bowie knife, and Harris pulled a pistol. The pistol misfired, but Harris had two guns. Duncan retreated when Harris produced his second pistol. Harris fired and killed Duncan, then galloped out of town ahead of the militia pursuit. He hid on his father's farm long enough for an attorney to be brought to him. Harris then rode back to town and surrendered to Sheriff Lewellyn. His trial resulted in acquittal on the expected grounds of self-defense.[25]

When the militia withdrew before the end of 1844, most Shelby County men still habitually carried guns but no one envisioned another general outbreak of violence. Shelby County had been overwhelmed by a 600-man army and by a caliber of leadership – Houston, Rusk, Smith, Horton, Broocks, Ochiltree, Roberts – that could not be matched in a rural county. However, if there would be no more general warfare, the Duncan-Harris fray indicated that individual hatreds still could erupt into bloodshed.

Watt Moorman was buried in this private cemetery atop a hill near his family home, which was downhill to the right. Bounded today by four posts, the little cemetery has ten unmarked graves. *(Photo by the author)*

# 11 Deadly Aftermath

*"The strife had been too long and
sharp for men's feelings of partiality and
prejudice to be suddenly eradicated."*
—Oran M. Roberts

When Colonel Alexander Horton rode into Shelby County with the militia in August 1844, he observed that "farms were left untilled growing in weeds." Horton was convinced that the fighting had been instigated by only a small minority. "Nearly all the men engaged in this deadly feud were small farmers, recent immigrants to Texas; most of them had been dragged into this by unscrupulous men." Regarding the Moderator force, Horton believed it "is highly probable that there were never a dozen bad men among them."[1]

Even if most of the combatants were farmers, they had joined the fight by instinct and inclination. Such Southern frontiersmen "were bound to come often into conflict," explained W.J. Cash in *The Mind of the South.* Men from the Southern backcountry and "the plantation world" were full of a "chip-on-the-shoulder swagger" that caused them to react directly to strife and affront – "conflict with them could only mean immediate physical clashing…."[2] After years of conflict and clashing in East Texas, such men could not easily cast aside the hard feelings, insults, and personal and property losses that had accumulated.

Lingering tensions meant that most men in Shelby County would continue to bear arms as a precaution. "Parties who visited Shelbyville still carried their guns," related Dr. Levi Ashcroft. Not long after Captain Len Mabbitt led his militia company back to

San Augustine, a court session in Shelbyville attracted a large crowd – and apparently every man carried pistols under his coat or in a pocket. In the courtroom a dispute broke out between a Regulator and a Moderator. Within an instant about twenty members of each faction whipped out their guns. Shooting was averted only by the quick action of the judge and the sheriff, who assembled an impromptu posse to arrest the adversaries.[3]

"Similar occurrences continued for more than a year afterwards," stated Dr. Ashcroft. Oran M. Roberts remarked that although Regulator-Moderator fighting had ended, "the spirit of enmity, though in modified form, still existed. The strife had been too long and sharp for men's feelings of partiality and prejudice to be suddenly eradicated." Former Regulator leader John Middleton had horses poisoned by old enemies.[4]

Before these strains and incidents could again explode into violence, important international events brought about an unexpected reconciliation between members of the two factions. During 1845 the United States and the Republic of Texas worked toward annexation and statehood, a process that was climaxed in a ceremony in Austin on February 19, 1846. After U.S. President James K. Polk made it clear that the southwestern boundary of the State of Texas would be the Rio Grande, rather than the traditional Nueces River, Mexico broke off diplomatic relations and ignored Polk's offer of $5 million in compensation. Polk's concurrent offers of $5 million for the vast but underpopulated area called New Mexico and up to $25 million for California also were rejected. President Polk ordered General Zachary Taylor to assemble an army at the mouth of the Nueces River. Fort Jesup was a major assembly point, although the 4,000-man force eventually sailed out of New Orleans for Texas.

War fever spread in Texas, where hostile feelings against Mexico remained strong. By May 1846 Taylor had moved his army to the north bank of the Rio Grande, where a detachment was attacked by a Mexican unit. Based on this incident, President Polk asked – and received – a declaration of war from Congress. Badly outnumbered, General Taylor requested reinforcements from the nearest source: two cavalry and two infantry regiments from the governor of Texas. A few companies of Texas Rangers already had joined Taylor, and now Texans enlisted by the thousands, including Governor James Pinckney Henderson, who received a leave of absence from the legislature to lead the Texas soldiers. Before the end of the War with Mexico, between five and seven thousand Texans served with the military.

East Texans eagerly formed volunteer companies. While San Augustine sent only a single company, sparsely settled Shelby County organized two cavalry companies, aggregating more than 135 men, in the spring of 1846. Captain M.T. Johnson, a Regulator leader, and Captain Alfred Truitt, a Moderator, each recruited an almost equal number of volunteers. Predictably, only Regulators or Regulator sympathizers joined Johnson's company – such as Eph and Charles Daggett, and John Myrick and Franklin Farrar, while Moderators – including four Truitts and three Dials -- enlisted in Truitt's company. The soldiers enrolled for six-month enlistments on Thursday, May 21, 1846, in Shelbyville. The two captains cooperated with a proper sense of military responsibility, as well as a growing personal friendship. Watt Moorman tried to enlist in the "Regulator" company, but Captain Johnson wisely declined the application of the former "Colonel Commandant." Moorman was so anxious to become part of the action that he attempted to join Truitt's company, but of course the arch-enemy of the Moderators was refused. Rebuffed by both companies, Moorman tagged along when the East Texans marched toward the scene of combat. Moorman dropped off in San Antonio, where he gambled and "frequented the Mexican fandangos every night...."[5]

The Shelby County men rode to Port Isabel, where they helped form the Second Texas Mounted Volunteers, a regiment commanded by Colonel George T. Wood. Captain M.T. Johnson's men were designated Company D, while Captain Truitt's company was Company I. The other companies were A from San Augustine; B from Liberty County; C from Harrison County; E from Nacogdoches; F from Harrison County; G from Rusk County; H from Crockett; and K from Sabine County. Regulator John Myrick,

First Sergeant of Company D, was elevated to lieutenant colonel of the Regiment.[6]

By the time the Second Texas Mounted Volunteers and other regiments reached Taylor, the veteran general known as "Old Rough and Ready" had defeated larger Mexican forces at the battles of Palo Alto and Resaca de la Palma. After receiving reinforcements, General Taylor marched with 6,600 of his men into Mexico toward the mountain city of Monterrey. The population of Monterrey was almost 15,000, and nearly 10,000 Mexican soldiers with artillery had prepared a defense.

Taylor's advance guard, including Texas Rangers led by Colonel Jack Hays, began fighting on September 19, 1846. For five days Taylor pressed his attack against another superior force. The long battle featured artillery duels and house-to-house fighting, and Lieutenant Ulysses Grant played a spectacular role as a volunteer courier. General Taylor coolly and aggressively commanded this complex combat, and the Mexicans surrendered on September 24. Like the other troops, the East Texans were exhausted and bedraggled and bloodied, but two days later they proudly formed up as the Mexican army marched out of the city.[7]

In October, with the six-month enlistments of the East Texans about to expire, General Taylor dissolved the Second Texas Mounted Volunteers. Major General Henderson also left the army and returned to his duties as governor, but the next year he refused to run for re-election. The election of 1847 was won by Colonel George T. Wood, in large part because of his wartime reputation. An even greater prize was won by another war hero, General Zachary Taylor, who was elected president of the United States in 1848.

In October 1846 some of the Shelby County men chose not to leave the army while the war still raged, and other East Texans also enlisted. Some, including Captain Truitt, who was promoted to major, served under Colonel Jack Hays. But most of the Shelby County men who had fulfilled their enlistment "were honorably discharged and returned home together," reported Dr. Ashcroft. He felt they had become "as warm friends as though they had never borne the appellation of Regulators and Moderators." Oran M.

Roberts concurred: "When they, as brother soldiers, returned home, the pacification was complete." The Shelby County warriors had endured the hardships of long marches and camp life and campaigning in a foreign land, as well as the hazards of a major battle. The camaraderie bred by these rugged adventures overcame earlier antagonisms.[8]

The returning heroes were welcomed home by a public banquet and ball in Shelbyville. Like countless other commanding officers, Colonel Wood and Governor Henderson – who was still in office and whose home was in nearby San Augustine – attended and both delivered speeches. There were "other distinguished persons" who also addressed the crowd, after which the dancing began. Former Regulators and Moderators "resolving to be friends, exchanged salutations as though nothing had ever occurred," reported Dr. Ashcroft. "With this public reunion passed away all traces of Regulating and Moderating…."[9]

After the war ended, in February 1848, Watt Moorman drifted back to Shelby County. "He had laid aside his haughty bearing and assumed instead a sullen, gloomy, bull dog air of insolent defiance." Dr. Ashcroft long had observed Moorman with deep disdain, and he noted that following the Mexican War, "he wandered about the country like an evil spirit, finding no resting place." Friendless and ostracized by the public, Moorman often left Shelby County. But he always gravitated back to the place where once he had been feared as he most powerful man in the county. Moorman took time to pen his version of the Regulator-Moderator War, regarded by John Middleton as the "only exactly, fair and true narrative" of the conflict that "was ever written." Regulator Middleton, of course, read Moorman's account with a biased eye. Unfortunately, the document "was destroyed or lost" before it could be preserved. Regardless of the viewpoint, the loss of a first-person account by the leader of the Shelby County Regulators is regrettable.[10]

Through his criminal contacts, Moorman secured the offer of a "large reward" to kidnap slaves in Texas and take them to dealers in Louisiana. Enlisting half a dozen desperados, Moorman traveled west to the Trinity River, stole a number of slaves, then led his party toward Louisiana. Hotly pursued, Moorman hid out in newly organized Panola County. When the search for him persisted, Moorman circulated a detailed account of his death. The pursuers finally returned to their homes and Moorman "made himself merry with his few remaining associates over the success of the ruse."[11]

Separated from his wife and little daughter, Moorman kept company with "a woman of bad character" known as Mrs. Wiseman. Her house was located north of Logansport on the east bank of the Sabine River, at the site of the old Watson's Ferry. Moorman lived with her for periods of time, but she also entertained other men. Mrs. Wiseman "was avoided by all virtuous women," and once she was given "a severe rebuke" by the wife of Dr. Robert Burns of Logansport. Enraged, Mrs. Wiseman intended to strike back, and in June 1849 she wrote to Dr. Burns, "threatening to destroy his reputation though she should forfeit her own, and even her life in the attempt."[12]

A few months later Mrs. Wiseman appeared before a Shelby County grand jury and charged that Dr. Burns had raped her one night in April 1848. An indictment was handed down, and even though he lived in Louisiana, Dr. Burns readily came to court in Shelbyville to prove his innocence. He produced the June letter, after which the respected James Truitt testified that he had spent the night in question at the home of Dr. Burns. The case was dismissed.

Enraged at this public humiliation, the volatile Mrs. Wiseman decided upon more drastic action. She obtained a brace of pistols and for a month practiced marksmanship under the tutelage of Watt Moorman. Early in 1850, Moorman and his paramour were standing on the wharf at Logansport awaiting the ferry. As the ferry approached from the Texas side, they recognized Dr. and Mrs. Burns. When the boat touched the wharf, Mrs. Wiseman stepped aboard and drew a pistol. Dr. Burns was armed with a double-barreled shotgun but was reluctant to shoot a woman. Instead he used his gun to deliver a blow to the side of her face. She sprawled unconscious onto the deck, and Dr. Burns took his wife's arm and

162

walked away. Watt Moorman was overheard muttering "that nothing saved Burns' life but his wife being with him." The double-barreled shotgun may also have contributed to Moorman's restraint.

Mrs. Wiseman decided to change tactics. A few days after her ill-fated attempt as a pistoleer, she heard that a Mrs. Parker, who lived in Shelby County a few miles from the Logansport ferry, would be attended in childbirth by Dr. Burns. She persuaded Moorman to commit another murder, and early the next morning Watt, aided by Mrs. Wiseman's seventeen-year-old son, set up an ambush site. Young Wiseman then went to the ferry to ask the ferryman, who lived in Logansport, to tell Dr. Burns that Mrs. Parker was in childbirth. Wiseman hurried back to help Moorman with the ambush.

Soon Dr. Burns appeared, riding a spirited horse. Anxious to reach his patient, he spurred his mount and the animal bolted – just as Moorman fired his rifle. The ball struck Dr. Burns' walking stick, sending a splinter into his hand. As soon as he was able to rein in his horse, Dr. Burns reached inside his coat for a pistol. But in his haste he had forgotten to arm himself, so he rode on toward Mrs. Parker's home, where he learned that she had not sent for him.

Realizing that he had been lured into a trap, Dr. Burns afterward was careful to remain armed and to stay on his guard, and he avoided other attempts to waylay him. Moorman finally enlisted the help of area ruffians and boasted of a new plan to kill Dr. Burns in Logansport. Dr. Burns was informed of Moorman's scheme by friends, and he decided upon a pre-emptive strike. The next morning, Thursday, February 14, 1850, Dr. Burns prepared the ultimate self-defense. His Logansport home overlooked the Sabine River, and he sat in a window with a spyglass trained on the Texas shore. About nine o'clock Dr. Burns sighted a heavily-armed Watt Moorman and two companions boarding the ferry.

Dr. Burns picked up his shotgun, which he had carefully loaded, and left the house. He walked purposefully to the main street, which led to the ferry landing. Dr. Burns stood at a corner where he could not be seen. Moorman and his friends disembarked and began to walk up the street, and Dr. Burns stepped out and began striding toward them.

The distance rapidly closed, and Moorman -- surprised and perhaps trying to readjust his plans in his mind -- failed to react. At about thirty paces Dr. Burns threw the shotgun to his shoulder and blasted Moorman with one barrel. The buckshot hurled Moorman to the ground. Dr. Burns quickly triggered the second barrel, but the load sailed above the falling Moorman. Stunned and mortally wounded, Moorman lay still for a moment. Then, somehow, the dying man stood up and brandished a pistol. Staggering forward a few steps, Moorman cursed Dr. Burns, then collapsed onto his face.

Still in his early thirties when he died, Watt Moorman was buried on a hill overlooking his father's home. There were few mourners and his grave remained unmarked, although nine other people are interred in what presumably was a family cemetery. The home cabin stood in the southern part of Panola County alongside a stream which then was known as Moorman Creek. There was a measure of poetic justice that Moorman was slain by the weapon most favored by participants of the Regulator-Moderator War. Familiar justice was obtained by Dr. Burns, who turned himself in to authorities at Mansfield, Louisiana, and was tried and acquitted on grounds of self-defense.

Watt Moorman was the last major figure of the Regulator-Moderator War to be killed. A year after Moorman died, one of his chief lieutenants, John Middleton, was hounded out of Shelby County. "I was so much annoyed by my enemies in Shelby county, by being waylaid, my horses poisoned, etc., and was kept so much disturbed that I left Shelby county in 1851...." Middleton raised hogs for a couple of years in Van Zandt County before moving to Parker County and later to Hood County, where he fought in numerous engagements against Native American raiders. Middleton had been wounded severely by Moderators, Comanche warriors inflicted other injuries, and eventually he lost the use of his left arm. His wife died in 1871; he remarried two years later and lived to write a history of his violent adventures in 1883. Middleton's autobiographical account makes it clear that, like other frontiersmen, he was always ready "to try my fortune in a new country," but persistent problems left over from the Regulator-Moderator War definitely influenced his decision to move away from Shelby County.[13]

While the camaraderie that developed during the War with Mexico was genuine, not everyone in Shelby County served in one of the two volunteer companies. Mexican War veterans may have pushed aside their old Regulator-Moderator hostilities, but many other citizens continued to harbor bitter feelings. The "new era of peace and good feeling"[14] proved not to be universal within Shelby County.

A woeful tragedy in 1847 was attributed to Regulator-Moderator hatreds. A Moderator partisan named Wilkerson hosted a wedding party at his home near East Hamilton. The bride was his adopted daughter. Nearly sixty people attended the dinner and most went into convulsions while eating. At least "eight or ten" died, and one report stated that Wilkerson "took this opportunity to destroy

Several victims of the "Poison Wedding" tragedy in 1847 are buried in the East Hamilton Cemetery. *(Photo by Karon O'Neal)*

as many Regulators as possible, to revenge himself for the injuries they had inflicted upon him and his friends." Supposedly he had arsenic mixed into the cakes, then warned the bride and other family members not to eat the confection. Wilkerson reportedly fled, but he was "captured and hung by a party of Regulators." There were fears that "the bloody feuds of the Regulators and Moderators may be renewed." Other speculations suggested that a disappointed suitor poisoned the party out of spite or that the cause was food poisoning in an unrefrigerated age. There has never been definitive proof, even of the number of dead, but in 1847 it was natural to blame the calamity on latent Regulator-Moderator hostility.[15]

Dr. Ashcroft related that many families left Shelby County during and after the Regulator-Moderator War. "The price of land decreased, farms with good substantial improvements were abandoned or disposed of at nominal prices and were suffered to grow up with weeds and briars and the houses to rot down." In addition to the departure of old citizens, newcomers to Texas, having heard of the war, "avoided the county as they could have done a city infested with the plague." Ashcroft lamented that "Shelbyville, once a flourishing little inland village, became almost deserted." Despite the rich lands, good timber, and pure water of Shelby County, "it has rather retrograded than improved. While her sister counties have increased in population and wealth she has stood a melancholy example of the evil effects of a resort to lynch law."[16]

Perhaps Dr. Ashcroft underestimated other factors which contributed to slow growth. No important roads bisected Shelby County; the closest was *El Camino Real,* too far south to impact Shelby County or, of course, Panola County, organized in 1846. The log cabin village of Pulaski remained the Panola County seat for a few years. Jonathan Anderson, one of twenty-five Moderators on Watt Moorman's proscribed list, moved to Panola County and donated land for a centrally located county seat. After Carthage was founded in 1848, Pulaski declined; no trace remains of the hamlet where Judge Hansford was intimidated by Charles Jackson and the Regulators. No railroad reached rural Panola County until 1888, and the population of Carthage remained under 1,000 until the twentieth century.

In 1866 an election transferred the seat of Shelby County from tiny Shelbyville to a new townsite named Center. The citizens of Shelbyville claimed that the election was fraudulent, but a few months later night raiders seized the county archives and brought them to the Center site in two ox carts. Without the seat of government, Shelbyville languished and the old courthouse burned. In 1884 the population of Shelbyville was no more than 150, and like Panola County, Shelby County remained rural and underpopulated. The Census of 1850 totaled 4,239 residents, with an increase to 5,362 in 1860. While these numbers represented a growth rate for Shelby County during the decade of almost twenty-five percent, the population of Texas nearly tripled from 1850 to 1860, from 212,592 to 604,215. Shelby County's growth during the years following the Regulator-Moderator

Jonathan and Jinsy Bittick, great-great-grandparents of the author. In 1835, when the Bitticks were in their thirties, they moved their family from Tennessee and were among the first settlers of future Shelby County. Jonathan was a miller whose home was located a few miles west of Shelbyville on Mill Creek. The Bitticks did not become involved in the Regulator-Moderator conflict, and remained in Shelby County after peace returned. They moved to a new frontier in the 1850s, settling in Williamson County. *(Author's photo)*

War, therefore, was quite modest when compared to the overall population explosion across Texas.

By contrast, Harrison County, where the Regulator-Moderator troubles began in 1840, enjoyed rapid growth and prosperity. During the 1850s the only railroad into Texas connected Marshall with Shreveport and linked Harrison County with the port of New Orleans by way of the Red River and the Mississippi River. A thriving cotton market and trade center, Marshall boasted antebellum homes, a brick courthouse, and a population of nearly 2,000 by 1860. There were almost 26,000 citizens countywide, including more slaves than any other county in Texas. Over 21,000 bales of cotton were produced in Harrison County in 1860, making it one of the wealthiest counties in antebellum Texas.

While cotton farmers and planters moved into Harrison County, some of the old settlers moved out of Shelby County. Like John Middleton, many wanted to leave the bitter and troublesome aftermath of the Regulator-Moderator War. Also like John Middleton, many were frontiersmen who restlessly sought fresh challenges.

Eph Daggett became a captain under Jack Hays during the Mexican War. In 1849 he ventured into West Texas and his brother Henry established a mercantile store at Fort Worth. By 1854 Eph also had moved his family to Fort Worth, along with another brother, Charles. Helen Daggett Moorman also moved to Fort Worth and remarried. Eph opened a hotel, drove cattle, and donated land for a railroad depot and right-of-way. The Daggetts, one of the backbone families of the Regulators in Shelby County, became important founders of Fort Worth, and an elementary school was named for Eph.[17]

Elihu and James Mauldin, ancestors of the author, moved from Tennessee in 1840 with family members, slaves, wagons, and equipment. Settling in Shelby County, they remained there through the Regulator-Moderator War, but moved west to Williamson County during the 1850s. Since they had endured the war years but were not active participants, it seems likely that the Mauldins left Shelby County primarily because they wanted to experience another frontier.[18]

Many families did remain in Shelby County. Moderator leader James Truitt won several elections to the state legislature, and so did his son Alfred, who rose to the rank of brigadier general during the Civil War. Sheriff Amon Lewellyn was elected to a succession of different county offices.[19] Others continued to farm their land, and so did their sons and grandsons.

These people, like the descendants of feudists everywhere, remained touchy about the old animosities. Regarding the Regulator-Moderator War, "for more than fifty years afterward the subject was tacitly avoided by the people of Shelby County, as tending to rouse again long-buried antagonisms and rekindle ancient hatred that had lain dormant through the years." Families in and around Shelbyville continued to express tensions related to Regulator-Moderator hostilities as recently as the mid-twentieth century.[20] Those who left Shelby County after the war moved on to new experiences and people, but many who continued to live among the old haunts of Regulators and Moderators found it difficult, if not to forgive, at least to forget.

Wyatt Earp was the central character in a blood feud between the Earp clan and the Clanton and McLaury brothers. The feud featured the most famous of all frontier shootouts, at Tombstone's OK Corral, and has been the subject of numerous films and novels. But the greatly overlooked Regulator-Moderator War produced three times as many casualties as did the Arizona gunfighters. *(Courtesy Arizona Historical Society)*

# 12 Legacy of a Blood Feud

*"'Vengeance is Mine!' saith the Lord.*
*But in and out of Texas He has*
*always had plenty of help."*
C.L. Sonnichsen, *Ten Texas Feuds*

Four years of Regulator-Moderator warfare, along with a lethal aftermath, produced more than thirty deaths – more than forty if the poisoned wedding is added to the toll. A sheriff, a senator, and a former district judge were killed. Violence included wilderness ambushes and skirmishes, lynchings and assassinations, street fights and pitched battles. By any measure, the Regulator-Moderator War of East Texas was a feud of major proportions, exceeding in number of participants and fatalities any similar conflict. But the Regulator-Moderator War failed to capture the public imagination, is only vaguely recalled today, and never has been recognized as the largest and most sanguinary of all nineteenth century feuds.

The most famous nineteenth-century feud pitted the Hatfields against the McCoys in the mountains of Kentucky and West Virginia. From 1878 until 1891 these two backwoods clans produced more than a dozen fatalities. But even though the Hatfields and McCoys became synonymous with feuding, the Regulators and Moderators of East Texas had proved far deadlier.[1]

Aside from the Regulator-Moderator strife, the bloodiest nineteenth-century feud was Arizona's Pleasant Valley War. This murderous clash between the Tewksbury and Graham families was triggered when the Tewksburys introduced sheep into cattle country. During 1887 and 1888, twenty-four men were killed, and at least one more was slain in retribution a few years later. Zane Grey wrote a novel, *To the Last Man,* based on this vicious range war, and the best-seller was filmed twice. Nevertheless, even the tragic body count of the Pleasant Valley War fell below that of the Regulator-Moderator War.[2]

More than fifteen men died in New Mexico's Lincoln County War during the 1870s and 1880s. The last casualty was Billy the Kid, who became a Western icon. Wyatt Earp and Doc Holliday also achieved iconic status through their blood feud with the Clanton-McLaury cattle rustling faction in and around Tombstone, Arizona, during the early 1880s. Three Earp brothers and Holliday killed three of their adversaries at Tombstone's OK Corral in a battle that became the West's most famous gunfight. Violent retributions followed which produced at least five more casualties, far below the grim total of the Regulators and Moderators. Billy the Kid, Wyatt, Doc, and the OK Corral captured the popular imagination to a degree never approached by the backwoods warriors of East Texas.[3]

In Wyoming during the 1890s, the Johnson County War erupted into the West's most infamous range conflict. Violence there included lynchings, ambushes, a heroic one-man stand, and a pitched battle involving hundreds of riflemen, all producing a dozen fatalities. Participants included the most prominent men in Wyoming, along with more than a score of hired gunmen from Texas. The Johnson County War inspired *The Virginian* and *Shane,* classic western novels which were adapted into major motion pictures.[4]

Part of the mystique which enveloped the Johnson County War, the Lincoln County War, the Earp troubles in Tombstone, and the Pleasant Valley War, as well as lesser feuds across the West, was the presence in each case of elements of the legendary post-Civil War cattle industry. There was no such popular connection – no participants named Earp or Holliday or Billy the Kid – with the Regulators and Moderators in East Texas during the 1840s.

Shelbyville will never resonate with the public like Tombstone, nor will Shelby County ever equate with Lincoln County. And Watt Moorman was no Wyatt Earp.

Even in Texas, the Regulator-Moderator War was overshadowed by lesser feuds in the late 1800s. Following the end of hostilities in East Texas, fully two decades passed before feuding broke out again. During the poisonous atmosphere of Reconstruction, the Early-Hasley feud pitted former Confederates against Union supporters in Bell County, where sporadic violence erupted from 1865 until 1869. The same causes triggered the Lee-Peacock feud, 1867-1871. The Sutton-Taylor feud broke out in 1869 in DeWitt County, apparently a resumption of a family enmity which had begun decades earlier in the Carolinas and Georgia. The notorious killer John Wesley Hardin, a native East Texan, fought alongside the Taylors, and in 1873 killed Sheriff Jack Helm, a leader of the Sutton "Regulators." Ambushes and street fights continued into the mid-1870s, with several victims on each side.[5]

Notorious killer John Wesley Hardin, the son of a Methodist circuit rider. Born and raised in East Texas, Hardin was the most dangerous gunman involved in the post-Civil War Sutton-Taylor feud. *(Author's collection)*

Texas was rife with lawlessness during the 1870s, and feuding was at its height. The Horrell-Higgins feud in Lampasas County pitted the Horrell brothers, rustlers and chronic troublemakers, against rancher-gunman Pink Higgins and his followers. Higgins killed one of the Horrell brothers in a Lampasas saloon, two others were lynched, and there was other violence in and around town. The Hoo Doo War, or Mason County War, was essentially a violent clash between Anglos and Germans, with the conflict aggravated by cattle theft.[6]

Lynching feuds in Shackleford County and in Bastrop County during the 1870s featured extralegal hangings triggered by cattle rustling and highway robberies and retributions. Vigilante justice in Bastrop County was aimed at a gang of thieves, and hangings continued into the 1880s. In Hood County the Mitchell and Truitt families feuded in 1874 over a land dispute, and two of the Truitts were wounded fatally. The next year Cooney Mitchell was hanged legally in Granbury. His son, Bill Mitchell, blamed the Rev. James Truitt, a young minister whose testimony had been a key to the conviction. In 1886, after nursing his grudge for more than a decade, Bill assassinated Truitt in his home at Timpson.

Texas feudist Pink Higgins. During the Horrell-Higgins War, Pink killed one Horrell brother and may have helped lynch two others. From a cracked tintype. *(Courtesy Betty L. Giddens)*

Over a quarter of a century later, the elusive Mitchell finally was imprisoned, but he escaped within two years.[7]

The Jaybird-Woodpecker War of Fort Bend County originated with efforts to control the black vote, then spread to include feuding families. The sheriff was killed during a wild shootout in front of the courthouse in Richmond in 1889. Feuding returned to the edge of Regulator-Moderator country at the turn of the century. The Wall-Border-Broocks feud exploded in San Augustine in 1900. Curg Border, a relative of the influential Broocks family, killed Sheriff George Wall, an old enemy, in the streets of San Augustine. Eugene Wall killed Ben Broocks in retaliation, followed by a gunbattle around the courthouse in which two more men were slain. After the Wall men were ambushed, a number of people left the country, following the pattern of the Regulator-Moderator War of sixty years earlier. Court action produced no convictions, but rough justice was meted out with a series of shootings, climaxing with the death of Curg Border at the hands of a new sheriff.[8]

There were numerous smaller feuds, and fatal conflicts continued into the twentieth century. Perhaps the most notable was the Johnson-Sims feud in Scurry and adjacent counties in 1916-1918. Billy Johnson was a wealthy Scurry County cattle rancher whose headstrong daughter, Gladys, married Ed Sims, son of a powerful Kent County rancher. Gladys and Ed had two daughters, but divorced in 1916. Following bitter custody disputes, Ed was shot to death by Gladys and her brother Sid in front of their father's bank in Snyder. Sid and Gladys were successfully defended in court by Judge Cullen Higgins, son of feudist Pink Higgins, and Gladys married famed Texas Ranger Frank Hamer.[9]

In the tradition of old-time feuds, the father of the murdered Ed Sims hired gunmen to extract blood vengeance. There was a foiled assassination attempt against Billy Johnson, followed by an assault in Sweetwater on Frank Hamer, who killed his primary assailant despite severe wounds. In 1918 a trio of assassins

Judge Cullen Higgins, oldest son of deadly gunman Pink Higgins. Suffering the same fate as another former district judge, John Hansford of the Regulator-Moderator War, Judge Higgins was assassinated during the Johnson-Sims feud in 1918. *(Author's collection)*

shotgunned Cullen Higgins, and after being arrested, one of the killers died at the hands of vengeful lawmen. Three-quarters of a century after Judge John Hansford was slain by East Texas Regulators, another former district judge was murdered during a West Texas feud.

A great many feuds erupted across Texas in the deadly wake of the Regulator-Moderator War. "At least a hundred of them might be totted up if the facts were all known," estimated Dr. C. L Sonnichsen, who knew more about Texas feuds than anyone else. There were more feuds in Texas than in any other state, and the first and largest of these conflicts, the Regulator-Moderator War, had a genesis effect on the feuds which came later. Referring to the Regulator-Moderator War, Dr. Sonnichsen stated flatly that "the pattern laid down in that terrible conflict became standard."[10]

In various Texas counties during the nineteenth century, citizens felt compelled to band together to quell rustlers, murderers, or other lawless ruffians. As in East Texas, the term "Regulators" sometimes was adopted. Lynching often resulted, at times with greater frequency than in East Texas during the 1840s. In some feuds sheriffs or judges were killed. Ambushes and street fights and assassinations were hallmarks of most feuds. These lethal tactics and devices were introduced to Texas on a large scale by Regulators and

Moderators during the 1840s. When feuding resumed in Texas after the Civil War, there was a large-scale precedent for vigilantism, lynching, impromptu gun battles, and the assassination of public officials. But even though the scores of post-Civil War feuds followed the pattern of the Regulator-Moderator War, none would approach the number of participants nor the grim total of fatalities amassed during the first and largest Texas vendetta.

For an event of such magnitude, historians have paid comparatively little attention to the Regulators and Moderators. "Authors of Texian history have, in some instances passed them over almost without notice," complained John Middleton in the little book he wrote about *Regulators and Moderators*. The first general *History of Texas,* written by Henderson Yoakum and published in 1855, ended with the annexation by the United States in 1846, and included nearly three pages on "the war of the `*Regulators*' and `*Moderators*.'" A *History of Texas, From 1685 to 1892* (1892), by John Henry Brown, reduced coverage of "THE EAST TEXAS FEUD" to a single page. Most twentieth century textbooks devote a paragraph to the Regulator-Moderator conflict. Many books have been published about Billy the Kid and the Lincoln County War, the Hatfields and McCoys, the Earps in Tombstone, and other feudists and feuds. But the largest of all feuds received almost no attention from researchers and publishers during the twentieth century.[11]

If historians – with the exception of C.L. Sonnichsen – have overlooked the Regulator-Moderator War, other storytellers have been inspired by this murderous strife, as bards have been attracted to armed conflicts through the ages. A long folk ballad about Robert Potter's murder began:

> Cans't tell me, Sir, of Potter bold,
> Of him betrayed and slain?
> If so, the story please unfold,
> And tell it o'er again.[12]

Another verse of "The Legend of Caddo Lake" was especially haunting:

> At night, beyond yon jutting cliff,
> Yon cliff upon the border,
> No fisherman will steer his skiff –
> There's blood upon the water![13]

In 1856 a New York publisher released a novel: *The Rangers and Regulators of the Tanaha: or, Life Among the Lawless. A Tale of the Republic of Texas.* The author was Judge A.W. Arrington, who had

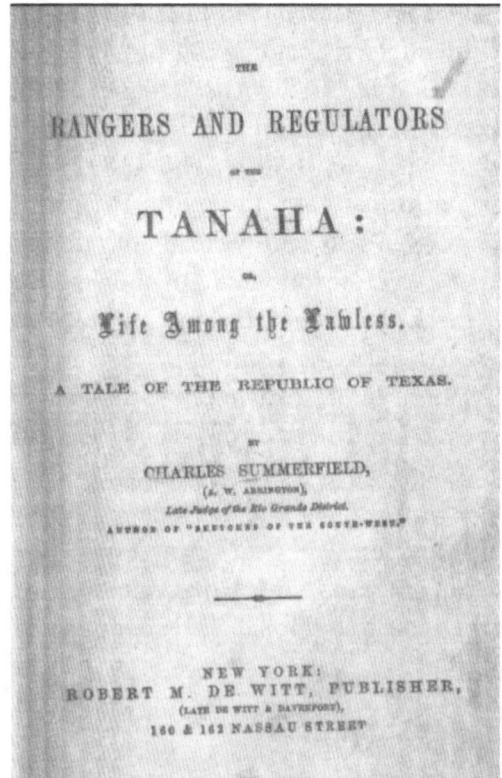

presided over the Rio Grande District of the Texas Republic. Judge Arrington began writing what his publisher called "popular works of adventure" with such titles as *The Scalp Hunters, Hunter's Feast,* and *The White Chief. The Rangers and Regulators of the Tanaha* was based on the Regulator-Moderator War, with which Judge Arrington was familiar. Writing only a few years after Watt Moorman was killed by Dr. Burns, Arrington expressed concern for the feelings of those who were still alive and for relatives

Title page of the blood-and-thunder novel based on the Regulator-Moderator War first published in 1856.

and friends of victims of the clash. "I was compelled, therefore, by motives of humanity, to exhibit the facts in the shape of a tale or story, indulging ... in a few of the liberties allowed by that species of composition."[14]

The author indulged in more than a few liberties. In a work of what later would be called historical fiction, there was far more fiction than history. Although the setting included Shelbyville and the Sabine River, the names of the men and women involved were changed, except for President Sam Houston and "Pete Whetstone, one of the most terrible desperadoes." Characters and events were altered and invented. The ugly and deformed "Comanche Ben" summoned "Roaring Dick" and other members of his "forest rangers" with a bugle instead of a hunting horn. The term "Lynchers" was substituted for Moderators. Dialogue was stilted and hopelessly melodramatic: "Oh, do not go, dearest father," breathed a girl whose brother – and his son – had just been slain. "They will butcher you as they did my poor brother Albert."[15]

*The Rangers and Regulators of the Tanaha* failed to create an audience for more literature about the Regulator-Moderator War. Besides, the pioneers who had lived through the conflict were too busy hacking a living from the wilderness to create verse or novels. Only four participants set down their memoirs at length. Regulator John Middleton wrote *A History of the Regulators and Moderators,* a forty-page book published in 1883 in Fort Worth. Three other first-person accounts remain unpublished. Less than a decade after the shooting stopped in East Texas, Dr. Levi Ashcroft wrote a lengthy account, "The History of the War Between the Regulators of Shelby County." Dr. Ashcroft moved his practice from Shelbyville to Tyler, and he died in 1855 before finding a publisher.

Another prominent Regulator, Eph Daggett, wrote a thirty-seven-page manuscript, "Recollections of the War of the Moderators and Regulators." When she was eighty-three and living with a daughter in New Orleans, Harriet Ames penned a beautifully written reminiscence, "The History of Harriet A. Ames During the Early

Days of Texas." Although Harriet's manuscript was never published, her dramatic and detailed account provided the material for a powerful novel.

Elithe Hamilton Kirkland, an experienced novelist, was shown a copy of Harriet's manuscript by Dr. H. Bailey Carroll, director of the Texas State Historical Association. She was captivated by the manuscript, as Dr. Carroll had anticipated. Kirkland dropped other projects and began researching and writing *Love is a Wild Assault,* published by Doubleday & Company in 1959. For more than 500 pages the author accompanies "Harriet through a lifetime of courageous living," focusing upon the heroine's adventures and romances in East Texas during the 1830s and 1840s.[16] *Love is a Wild Assault* features a great deal of melodramatic romance, but the historical background, rich with reliable detail, is an important part of the book. The novel inspired a one-woman play, *Texian Woman, A Dramatization,* by Marcia Thomas.

The public reservoir of memories about the Regulator-Moderator War is not very deep: a ballad; two novels written more than a century apart; a few personal reminiscences; and a one-woman play. There is no statue of Robert Potter in Amarillo, the seat of Potter County, although there is an appropriate marker at his gravesite in the State Cemetery in Austin. The most impressive monument to a participant is the tall obelisk in Scottsville which marks the grave of Potter's arch-enemy, William P. Rose. There is a handsome monument to Harriet Ames at Potter's Point, and historical markers stand outside Shelbyville and at the hard-to-reach Pulaski townsite. The museums that house archival materials about the conflict have no artifacts on display.

C.L. Sonnichsen derived the title to his first book about Texas feuds, *I'll Die Before I'll Run,* from a Smoky Mountain ballad:

Wake up, wake up, darlin' Corie!
And go get me my gun.
I ain't no hand for trouble,
But I'll die before I'll run.

Certainly this ballad reflects the stubborn bravery of the feudists of Shelby and Harrison counties. Some East Texans did run, of course, moving with their families away from the Regulator-Moderator fighting, but most clung to their wilderness homes even though they had possessed their land only a few years. Like settlers on every frontier, East Texans were tenacious in the face of danger and had no intention of giving up their property. House burnings, lynchings, shootings, and the relentless lust for vengeance were lamentable products of the Regulator-Moderator War.

During four years of ambushes and hangings, murders and battles, there also were numerous displays of heroism, endurance, and sheer physical courage by both men and women – qualities which were essential for the conquest of the continent. Beyond the individual attributes and deeds which inspire admiration, the Regulator-Moderator War was a landmark event in the history of extralegal violence. Nothing is more dramatic than a life or death conflict, and it is time to recognize the high drama, the "thrilling and tragical events"[17] enacted and endured by the Regulators and Moderators of old East Texas.

# R.I.P.
## Victims of the Regulator-Moderator War

1840    George W. Rembert, *shot by Moderators*
       Isaac Hughes, *shot by Moderators*
1841    Sheriff John B. Campbell, *assassinated by Regulators*
       Daniel Minor, *killed by Regulators*
       D. Morriss, *killed by Regulators*
       Joseph Goodbread, *shot by Charles Jackson*
       Charles Jackson, *assassinated*
       _____ Lour, *line of fire*
       _____ Bledsoe, *shot during fight with Regulators*
       Bill McFadden, *hanged by mob*
       John McFadden, *hanged by mob*
       Squire Humphries, *hanged by Regulator posse*
1842    Robert Potter, *shot by Regulator John Scott*
       _____Boatright, *shot by Regulators*
       Tiger Jim Strickland, *shot*
       Farrar Metcalf, *shot*
       Henry Strickland, *brained*
1843    Samuel N. Hall, *shot by Stanfield*
       _____Stanfield, *lynched by Regulators*
       Peter Whetstone, *shot by Regulator Wm. Boulware*
1844    Judge John Hansford, *killed by Regulator posse*
       Henry Runnells, *murdered by Moderator assassins*
       William Wells Williams, *hanged by Regulators*
       James Hall, *assassinated by Regulators*
       John Bradley, *shot by Watt Moorman*
       Bill Hansbury, *killed at Beauchamp's*
       Capt. George Davidson, *killed at Church Hill*
       Howell Hudson, *killed at Church Hill*
       _____Kane, *killed at Church Hill*
       Vardeman Duncan, *shot by Moderator in street fight*
1847    Wedding party, *poisoned by Moderator for revenge*
1850    Watt Moorman, *shotgunned by Dr. Burns*

# Endnotes

Formal citations of each of the noted sources are contained in the Bibliography.

**CHAPTER ONE:**  Murder in Shelbyville
[1] Ashcroft ms, 32-34.
[2] Daggett ms, 6-9.
[3] Ashcroft ms, 35; Daggett ms, 9-10.
[4] Daggett ms, 9.
[5] Daggett ms, 9-10.
[6] Daggett ms, 10.
[7] This account of the shooting is taken from Daggett ms, 10-22 and Ashcroft ms, 33-34.
[8] An extensive history of extralegal violence was presented by Richard Maxwell Brown in *Strain of Violence, Historical Studies of American Violence and Vigilantism.* Also see Frank Richard Prassel, *The Great American Outlaw, A Legacy of Fact and Fiction;* W. Eugene Hollon, *Frontier Violence, Another Look;* and Wayne Guard, *Frontier Justice.*
[9] Brown, *Strain of Violence,* 59-60.
[10] Brown, *Strain of Violence,* 95, 113, 115.
[11] Brown, *Strain of Violence,* 97, 105-06, 126-27, 163-67.
[12] Ashcroft ms, 3.

**CHAPTER TWO:**  Regulator-Moderator Country
[1] Quote vigorously cited to the author by Linda Freeman, museum curator at Fort Jesup.
[2] Malone, ed., *A. Horton,* 35.
[3] *Redlander,* October 21, 1841.
[4] Horgan, "The Lost Journal of a Southwestern Frontiersman," *Southwestern Historical Quarterly* ( XLIV, July 1940), 1.
[5] Horgan, "The Lost Journal of a Southwestern Frontiersman," *SWHQ* (XLIV, July 1940), 1.
[6] For details and overviews of the weapons and ammunition discussed in this segment, see Boorman, *Guns of the Old West,* and Worman, *Gunsmoke and Saddle Leather.*
[7] Daggett ms, 28.
[8] Daggett ms, 19.
[9] Ames ms, 52.
[10] Ames ms, 41.
[11] Daggett ms, 9-10.

[12]Middleton, Regulators and Moderators, 23.
[13]Daggett ms, 46.

**CHAPTER THREE:** Jackson's Regulators
[1]Cited in Whitfield pamphlet, 1.
[2]Ashcroft ms, 55.
[3]Ashcroft ms, 36.
[4]Related to the author by Gilbert Garrett at the 180-year-old Garrett cabin, November 17, 2005.
[5]Middleton, *Regulators and Moderators,* 8.
[6]Ashcroft ms, 4-8, 12-13.
[7]Ashcroft ms, 9-11.
[8]Ashcroft ms, 16-17; Middleton, *Regulators and Moderators,* 8-9.
[9]Ashcroft ms, 33.
[10]Middleton, *Regulators and Moderators,* 16; Daggett ms, 11; Ashcroft ms, 36.
[11]Details of this incident are provided by Eph Daggett in his manuscript, 11-12.
[12]Ashcroft ms, 36.
[13]Middleton, *Regulators and Moderators,* 13.
[14]Daggett ms, 18-19.
[15]Daggett ms, 5-6; Middleton, *Regulators and Moderators,* 15.
[16]Daggett ms, 15-17, 47.
[17]Ashcroft ms, 37.
[18]The only detailed account of the raid on the Strickland and McFadden homes is in the Ashcroft ms, 36-37.
[19]Blake, "John M. Hansford," *New Handbook of Texas,* Vol. 3, 444; Daggett ms, 22.
[20]Ashcroft ms, 37; Daggett ms, 22.
[21]Daggett ms, 22; *Marshall News-Messenger,* November 10, 1963.
[22]Ashcroft ms, 38; the letters to the sheriff and court clerk are in *Harrison County District Court, Civil Minutes,* 64, and also are reproduced in Judge Whitfield's pamphlet, 1-2, and in the Marshall *News-Messenger,* November 10, 1963.
[23]*Marshall News-Messenger,* November 10, 1963; Daggett ms, 23; for the articles of impeachment, see *Journals, Sixth Congress, Republic of Texas, 1841-42,* Vol. I, 207-209.
[24]Ashcroft ms, 38; *Marshall News-Messenger,* November 10, 1963.
[25]Ashcroft ms, 38; Daggett ms, 22-23.

**CHAPTER FOUR:** Watt Moorman
[1]Middleton, *Regulators and Moderators,* 13, 16.
[2]Ashcroft ms, 41; Middleton, *Regulators and Moderators,* 16.

[3] Middleton, *Regulators and Moderators,* 16-17; Ashcroft ms, 41.

[4] Ashcroft ms, 42; Middleton, *Regulators and Moderators,* 16.

[5] Ashcroft ms, 42-43; Middleton, *Regulators and Moderators,* 16.

[6] Middleton, *Regulators and Moderators,* 8, 17.

[7] Middleton, *Regulators and Moderators,* 17; Daggett ms, 13.

[8] Middleton, *Regulators and Moderators,* 17. Middleton relates the story of the ensuing fight and surrender, and the trip back to Shelbyville.

[9] Middleton, *Regulators and Moderators,* 17; Daggett ms, 13.

[10] Middleton provides the only detailed account of the return from Montgomery through Crockett and on to Shelbyville. *Regulators and Moderators,* 18-19.

[11] Middleton, *Regulators and Moderators,* 19; Daggett ms, 13-14; Ashcroft ms, 45.

[12] Ashcroft ms, 45-46.

[13] Daggett ms, 14.

[14] Ashcroft ms, 46.

[15] Daggett ms, 23-24; Ashcroft ms, 44.

[16] Ashcroft ms, 43-44; Daggett ms, 23-24.

[17] Ashcroft ms, 43-44, 56; Daggett ms, 23-24.

[18] Daggett ms, 14-15.

[19] Daggett ms, 14.

[20] Ashcroft ms, 46.

[21] Sanders, ed. "A Letter From East Hamilton, Texas." *ETHJ,* 47.

[22] Horgan, "The Lost Journal of Southwestern Frontiersman," *SWHQ,* 9.

**CHAPTER FIVE:** War in Harrison County

[1] The biographical entry on William Pinckney Rose in *The New Handbook of Texas,* Vol. 5, 679, was written by Margaret Stoner McLean, great-great-granddaughter of Rose. Other biographical information is available in McLean, "A Famous Murder of 1842, Rose-Potter," *Texas Methodist Historical Quarterly* (II, No. 1, July 1910), 1-11. Also see the vertical file on Rose at the Harrison County Historical Society in Marshall, and White, *1840 Citizens of Texas, Land Grants,* Vol. III, 245.

[2] For the killings of Rembert and Hughes, see McLean, "Rose, William Pinckney, New Handbook of Texas, Vol. 5, 679; and McLean, "A Famous Murder of 1842," TMHQ, 9.

[3] White, *1840 Citizens of Texas, Land Grants,* Vol. 3, 44; District Officers, Vertical File, Harrison County Historical Society.

[4] District Officers, Vertical File, Harrison County Historical Society; McLean "A Famous Murder of 1842," *TMHQ,* Vol. II, 9.

[5] District Officers, Vertical File, Harrison County Historical Society; White, *1840 Citizens of Texas, Land Grants,* Vol. 3, 199 and 205.

[6]Related to the author by Judge Ben Z. Grant, president of the Harrison County Historical Association, on November 15, 2005, in Marshall. The story is preserved in Armstrong, "The History of Harrison County, Texas, 1839 to 1880," M.A. Thesis, Stephen F. Austin State Teachers College 108.

[7]There are two biographies of Robert Potter: Ernest G. Fischer, *Robert Potter, Founder of the Texas Navy*, published in 1976; and Ernest C. Shearer, *Robert Potter, Remarkable North Carolinian and Texan*, 1951. Harriet Moore Gage (Potter) Ames recorded excellent insights and details about Potter in her memoirs, and other information is available in Potter's biographical files in the archives of the Jefferson County Historical Museum and the Harrison County Historical Museum in Marshall. The sketch of Potter in this chapter is drawn from these sources, which agree on almost all points. Quotations from these sources are footnoted.

[8]Ames, "Harriet Ames," 37. For a summary of her life, see McArthur, "Ames, Harriet A. Moore Page Potter, *New Handbook of Texas*, Vol. 1, 152-153

[9]Ames, "Harriet Ames," 21.

[10]Houston speech, transcribed in *Galveston Weekly News*, June 19, 1855. William and Barker, eds., *Writings of Sam Houston*, Vol. VI, 190.

[11]Ames, "Harriet Ames," 26-27.

[12]Ames, "Harriet Ames," 37.

[13]Harriet's lyrical description of her lovely homesite is on pages 34 through 36 of her manuscript.

[14]Claude McCrocklin of Shreveport, who performed an archaeological excavation of the Potter homesite, provided the author with a thorough report which reveals many details about the house and outbuildings.

[15]Kemp, *Signers of the Texas Declaration of Independence*, 277.

[16]Shearer, *Robert M. Potter*, 95; *Houston Morning Star*, July 13, 1842.

[17]Ames, "Harriet Ames," 45-46.

[18]Ames, "Harriet Ames," 46-47.

[19]The only first-person account of the death of Robert Potter was left by Harriet Ames, on pages 48-54 of her manuscript. Virtually all subsequent accounts have been based on Harriet's description.

[20]McLean, Reminiscences, 35

[21]Harriet told of finding Potter's body, and the subsequent burial, on pages 54-55.

[22]*Marshall News-Messenger*, June 13, 1937.

[23]Documents cited in Shearer, *Robert Potter*, 100; Ames, "Harriet Ames," 58-62.

[24] Kemp, *Signers of the Texas Declaration of Independence*, 277.

[25]Fischer, *Robert Potter*, 218; Ames, "Harriet Ames," 63-64; McLean, Reminiscences, 19-20.

[26]The best collection of information about Whetstone is in his bio-

graphical file in the Harrison County Historical Society, Marshall.

[27]Daggett ms, 21. Whetstone's sons were Anderson (age twenty in 1840, when the feuding commenced), Warrick (fifteen years of age in 1840), and Johnston (six in 1840). Another son had died at the age of four, and there were two daughters. Johnston Whetstone was too young to participate in the Regulator-Moderator War, so Anderson and Warrick must have been the "good fighters" sent by their father "down into Shelby County to fight the Regulators." From a photocopied page of the 1835 Census Report of the Sabine, and the Census of 1850 in Whetstone's biographical file at the Harrison County Historical Society.

[28]Accounts of Whetstone's pursuit and death at the hands of Boulware are in: Armstrong, "The History of Harrison County, Texas, 1839 to 1880," M.A. Thesis, 109; Marshall *News-Messenger,* May 9, 1965, and June 13, 1972; pamphlet by Judge T. Davidson Whitfield in biographical file of Robert Potter, Harrison County Historical Society; *Telegraph and Texas Register,* December 13, 1843.

[29]Daggett ms, 23.

[30]Blake, "Hansford, John M." *New Handbook of Texas,* Vol. 3, 444; Marshall *News-Messenger*, November 10, 1963.

[31]Ames, "Harriet Ames," 69.

[32]Fischer, *Robert Potter*, 220-227.

[33]Ames, "Harriet Ames," 71.

[34]Ames, "Harriet Ames," 26.

**CHAPTER SIX:** Regulator Ascendancy

[1]The petition was dated December 18, 1841. Quoted in Love, "The Regulator-Moderator Movement," Thesis, 60-61.

[2]Ashcroft described Moorman's heavy-handed control of the county and of Shelbyville on pages 48-50 of his manuscript.

[3]For the Boatright incident, see Ashcroft ms, 46-47.

[4]Ashcroft ms, 55-56.

[5]Henderson, "Ochiltree, William Beck." *New Handbook of Texas,* Vol. 4, 1103.

[6]A detailed account of the Judge Ochiltree's appearance at the Shelbyville courthouse is in the Ashcroft ms, 51.

[7]Middleton, in *Regulators and Moderators,* 19-20, relates his wounding and convalescence.

[8]Daggett ms, 16; Middleton, *Regulators and Moderators,* 20.

[9]Daggett ms, 16-17.

[10]Dr. Ashcroft knew the Daggett family well, and discussed the union between Helen and Moorman on pages 54-55 of his manuscript.

[11]Daggett ms, 36.

[12]Ashcroft ms, 54-55.

### CHAPTER SEVEN: Of Hogs and Men

[1]Ashcroft ms, 59.

[2]Dr. Ashcroft, on pages 59-63 of his manuscript, provides the only detailed account of the murder of Samuel Hall, and the pursuit of his killer.

[3]Nix, *Shelby County – Part of Her Early Story*, 23.

[4]Williams confession in Sanders, ed., Hangings in Shelby County, 2-3.

[5]Martin, "Bradley, John M." *New Handbook of Texas*, Vol. 1, 694; Malone, ed., *Alexander Horton*, 37; Daggett ms, 37; John Middleton, *Regulators and Moderators*, 20.

[6]Williams confession.

[7]In addition to the Williams confession, the Runnels killing is related, with considerable agreement in: Ashcroft ms, 64-65; Daggett ms, 37-38; Middleton, *Regulators and Moderators*, 20-21.

[8]Daggett ms, 38-39; Middleton, *Regulators and Moderators*, 21.

[9]The author was shown the site of the Brinson blockhouse by Johnny Hargrove on January 17, 2006.

[10]Ashcroft ms, 66; Middleton, *Regulators and Moderators*, 21.

[11]Ashcroft ms, 67, 69; Daggett ms, 39-40.

[12]Ashcroft ms, 67-68; Middleton, *Regulators and Moderators*, 21; "A.F.," Letter to the Editor, *San Augustine Redlander*, reproduced in Sanders, ed., Hangings in Shelby County, 1-2.

[13]Daggett ms, 40-41; Ashcroft ms, 65. Daggett related the testimony of Hall, while Dr. Ashcroft recorded the pleas of Mrs. Hall.

[14]The pursuit of Stanfield through Mississippi and Arkansas, is related in Ashcroft ms, 61-63, 68.

[15]Daggett ms, 41.

[16]Ashcroft ms, 69-70.

[17]Ashcroft ms, 75-76.

[18]Ashcroft ms, 76.

[19]Ashcroft ms, 71-72. John Middleton *(Regulators and Moderators, 21)* claimed that 300 Moderators assembled at the Todd blockhouse, but that total seems far too high at this stage of events.

[20]Ashcroft ms, 72-73; Middleton, *Regulators and Moderators*, 21.

[21]The Moorman letter is preserved by Dr. Ashcroft in his manuscript, 73.

[22]Ashcroft ms, 73-74.

[23]Bradley's move to San Augustine and his murder are related by Col. Alexander Horton, a prominent citizen of the community, in Malone, ed., *Alexander Horton*, 37-38. Also providing useful accounts of this startling event are: Ashcroft ms, 81-85; Daggett ms, 25-27; Middleton, *Regulators and Moderators*, 26-27; *Clarksville Northern Standard*, August 7, 1844.

24Ashcroft ms, 82-83.

25Malone, ed., *Alexander Horton,* 37-38; Ashcroft ms, 84.

26Ashcroft ms, 85.

27Ashcroft ms, 85.
28Daggett ms, 27.

**CHAPTER EIGHT:** Mobilization
[1]Ashcroft ms, 77.
[2]Ashcroft ms, 78-79.
[3]Ashcroft ms, 79-80.
[4]Cited in Ashcroft ms, 80.
[5]Cited in Love, "The Regulator-Moderator Movement," Thesis, 78-80.
[6]Ashcroft ms, 86.
[7]Ashcroft ms, 89.
[8]Daggett ms, 27; Malone, ed., *Alexander Horton*, 36.
[9]Middleton, *Regulators and Moderators,* 22.
[10]Middleton, *Regulators and Moderators,* 25; Ashcroft ms, 22.
[11]Ashcroft ms, 92-94, 127.
[12]Daggett ms, 27-28.
[13]Daggett ms, 28.
[14]Daggett ms, 28. Daggett said that there were eighteen men on the list, but Dr. Ashcroft listed twenty-five names, and other sources agreed that there were twenty-five. Ashcroft ms, 95-96; Middleton, *Regulators and Moderators*, 21; Malone, ed., *Alexander Horton*, 35.
[15]Ashcroft ms, 98, 100.
[16]Ashcroft ms, 98-99; Daggett ms, 29.
[17]Ashcroft ms, 100-101.
[18]Ashcroft ms, 100, 102.
[19]Ashcroft ms, 98, 101, 10

**CHAPTER NINE:** Battle
[1]Ashcroft ms, 102; Middleton, *Regulators and Moderators*, 23.
[2] Ashcroft ms, 102-103; Middleton, *Regulators and Moderators,* 22.
[3]O'Neal, *Tex Ritter*, 3-4.
[4] Ashcroft ms, 103.
[5] Ashcroft ms, 103-104.
[6]Daggett ms, 29.
[7] Middleton, *Regulators and Moderators*, 22,
[8] Ashcroft ms, 104.
[9] Middleton, *Regulators and Moderators,* 22; Daggett ms, 29-30; Ashcroft ms, 104. These three men, two Regulators and one Moderator, described the battle in detail.
[10]Daggett ms, 30.
[11]Daggett ms, 31.
[12]Daggett ms, 31.
[13]Ashcroft ms, 105.

[14]Middleton, *Regulators and Moderators,* 23.
[15]Daggett ms, 32; Ashcroft ms, 105.
[16]Middleton, *Regulators and Moderators,* 23.
[17]Malone, ed., *Alexander Horton,* 36.
[18] Middleton, *Regulators and Moderators,* 23.
[19]Ashcroft ms, 106.
[20]Ashcroft ms, 106-107; Middleton, *Regulators and Moderators,* 23-24.
[21]Ashcroft ms, 107.
[22]Middleton, *Regulators and Moderators,* 24.
[23]Daggett ms, 32.
[24]Middleton, *Regulators and Moderators,* 24.
[25]Middleton, *Regulators and Moderators,* 24; Ashcroft ms, 108; Daggett ms, 32.
[26]Ashcroft ms, 109; Middleton, *Regulators and Moderators,* 24.
[27]Daggett ms, 32.
[28]Ashcroft ms, 111-112.
[29]Middleton, *Regulators and Moderators,* 24.
[30]Daggett ms, 32-33.
[31]Middleton, *Regulators and Moderators,* 24; Ashcroft ms, 110. Dr. Ashcroft said the fighting "continued in all about two hours," while John Middleton thought the "action continued about four hours."
[32]Daggett ms, 33; Ashcroft ms, 110; Malone, ed., *Alexander Horton,* 36.
[33]Ashcroft ms, 110.
[34]Ashcroft ms, 112.
[35]Daggett ms, 33; Malone, ed., *Alexander Horton,* 36; Roberts, "The Shelby War," *Texas Magazine,* 14, 16; Ashcroft ms, 112.
[36]Middleton, *Regulators and Moderators,* 24-25.
[37]Middleton, *Regulators and Moderators,* 25; Ashcroft ms, 113.
[38]Ashcroft ms, 113.
[39]Ashcroft ms, 114.
[40]Ashcroft ms, 114.
[41]Ashcroft ms, 114-115; Middleton, *Regulators and Moderators,* 25.
[42]Ashcroft ms, 116-119. Dr. Ashcroft provides the only detailed account of the maneuvers at this stage of the Moderators and Regulators.
[43]Ashcroft ms, 120-121.
[44]Daggett ms, 33-34. Daggett gives a first person account of this incident.

**CHAPTER TEN:** Houston and the Militia
[1]Roberts, "The Shelby War," *Texas Magazine,* 13-14.
[2]Ashcroft ms, 95.
[3]San Augustine *Redlander,* August 17, 1844; Roberts, "The Shelby War," *Texas Magazine,* 16-17.

[4]This proclamation may be found in Ashcroft ms, 120-121; and Crocket, *Two Centuries in East Texas,* 199-200.

[5]Ashcroft ms, 121-122; Bradley, ed., *A. Horton,* 38.

[6]Daggett ms, 34.

[7] Daggett ms, 34; Middleton, *Regulators and Moderators,* 26; Ashcroft ms, 122.

[8]Williams and Barker, eds. *The Writings of Sam Houston,* Vol. IV, 361-362.

[9]Williams and Barker, eds. *The Writings of Sam Houston,* Vol. IV, 361-367. The correspondence cited in the text is within these pages in chronological order.

[10]Middleton, *Regulators and Moderators,* 26; Ashcroft ms, 122.

[11]Middleton, *Regulators and Moderators,* 26. Middleton is the only source for Hudson's burial and his party's subsequent experiences.

[12]Ashcroft ms, 123-125; Daggett ms, 34-35.

[13]Ashcroft ms, 123, 125-126; Middleton, *Regulators and Moderators,* 26.

[14]Daggett ms, 35; Malone, ed., *A. Horton,* 38.

[15]Houston to Smith, August 23, 1844. Williams and Barker, eds. *The Writings of Sam Houston,* Vol. IV, 365-366.

[16]Houston to Smith, August 23, 1844, 9 o'clock p.m.; Houston to Smith, August 26, 1844. Williams and Barker, eds. *The Writings of Sam Houston,* Vol. IV, 366-367.

[17]Roberts, "The Shelby War," *Texas Magazine,* 18; Ashcroft ms, 134; Crocket, *Two Centuries in East Texas,* 224.

[18]Malone, ed. *A. Horton,* 38; Roberts, "The Shelby War," *Texas Magazine*, 18; Ashcroft ms, 127. Local lore in Shelbyville relates that Sam Houston addressed the Regulator-Moderator prisoners in an oak grove just east of the courthouse square. But all contemporary accounts place the prisoners and Houston and his address in San Augustine. It is also believed locally that Houston made a political speech in Shelbyville during one of his many campaigns for office, an appearance which may have become confused with his Regulator-Moderator address.

[19]Ashcroft ms, 127.

[20]Ashcroft ms, 128-129; San Augustine *Redlander,* September 7, 1844; Michael Moorman Fricke provided information about his notorious ancestor, as well as Watt's wife and daughter, in Watt Moorman's biographical article in *The New Texas Handbook,* Vol. IV, 828.

[21]Malone, ed., *A. Horton,* 38; Ashcroft ms, 130; San Augustine *Redlander,* October 3, 1844.

[22]Ashcroft ms, 130-131.

[23]Ashcroft ms, 132-133.

[24]Ashcroft ms, 133; Roberts, "The Shelby War," *Texas Magazine,* 18.

[25]Middleton, *Regulators and Moderators,* 26; Ashcroft ms, 134.

**CHAPTER ELEVEN:** Deadly Aftermath

[1]Bradley, ed. *A. Horton,* 35-36.

[2]Cash, *The Mind of the South,* 44-45.

[3]Ashcroft ms, 134-135.

[4]Ashcroft ms, 135; Roberts, "The Shelby War," *Texas Magazine,* 19; Middleton, *Regulators and Moderators,* 27.

[5]Ashcroft ms, 136; Crocket, *Two Centuries in East Texas,* 202-203.

[6]Bennie Nix compiled a little volume listing names and giving enlistment dates, ages, ranks and promotions, and details about equipment, horses, and illnesses of the *Soldiers Serving From Shelby County in 1846 – 1848.*

[7]For the Battle of Monterrey see: Esposito, ed. *West Point Atlas of American Wars,* Vol. I, map 14b and accompanying description; Nevin, *The Mexican War,* 64-79; Nichols, *Zach Taylor's Little Army,* 105, 133-182.

[8]Ashcroft ms, 137; Roberts, "The Shelby War," *Texas Magazine,* 19.

[9]Ashcroft ms, 137.

[10]Ashcroft ms, 236, 138; Middleton, *Regulators and Moderators,* 5.

[11]Ashcroft ms, 139.

[12]Ashcroft ms, 140-156. Dr. Ashcroft provides the most detailed account of the clash between Dr. Burns, Mrs. Wiseman, and Watt Moorman. Also see Michael Moorman Friske, "Moorman, Charles Watt," *New Handbook of Texas,* Vol. IV, 828.

[13]Middleton, *Regulators and Moderators,* 8, 27.

[14]Crocket, *Two Centuries in East Texas,* 202.

[15]*Niles' Weekly Register,* May 22, June 5 and 19, 1847; Houston *Telegraph and Texas Register,* May 1847, articles copied by Annette Sanders Person, and provided to the author by Bob Bowman. Also see Bowman's account of the tragedy in *More Historic Murders of East Texas,* 18-27.

[16]Ashcroft ms, 157-158.

[17]Sanders, *How Forth Worth Became the Texasmost City,* 13, 15, 16, 18, 20, 26, 35, 41.

[18]Mauldin genealogical records in the possession of the author, and of other family members.

[19]A complete list of Shelby County office holders may be found in Nix, *Shelby County.*

[20]Crocket, *Two Centuries in East Texas,* 202; Johnny Hargrove, a lifelong resident of Shelbyville, related to the author tensions experienced during the 1950s, more than a century after the war.

**Chapter Twelve:** Legacy of a Blood Feud

[1]For the Hatfield-McCoy feud, see Rinaldi, *The Coffin Quilt,* and Jones, *The Hatfields and the McCoys.*

[2]See Forrest, *Arizona's Dark and Bloody Ground;* Dedera, *A Little War of Our Own;* and O'Neal, *Cattlemen vs. Sheepherders,* 43-65.

[3]Literature is prolific on Billy the Kid and the Lincoln County War, and on Wyatt Earp, Doc Holliday and the OK Corral.

[4]O'Neal, *The Johnson County War*

[5]These Texas feuds were explored by C.L. Sonnichsen in *I'll Die Before I'll Run* and *Ten Texas Feuds.* Sonnichsen, the greatest authority on Texas feuding, featured the Regulator-Moderator War in *Ten Texas Feuds.*

[6]For the Horrell-Higgins feud, see Nolan, *Bad Blood,* and O'Neal, *Pink Higgins.* For the Mason County War, see Johnson, *The Mason County "Hoo Doo" War.*

[7]Sonnichsen, *I'll Die Before I'll Run* and *Ten Texas Feuds.*

[8]Sonnichsen, *I'll Die Before I'll Run,* explores both the Jaybird-Woodpecker War and the Wall-Border-Broocks feud. For the latter feud, also see Combs, *Gunsmoke in the Redlands.*

[9]For the Johnson-Sims feud, see O'Neal, *Pink Higgins,* 103-156.

[10]Sonnichsen, *Ten Texas Feuds,* 5, 7.

[11]Middleton, *A History of Regulators and Moderators,* 15; Yoakum, *History of Texas,* 438-440; Brown, *History of Texas, From 1685 to 1892,* 295. Textbooks consulted: Eugene C. Barker, *A School History of Texas,* 1913; J.L. Clark, *A History of Texas, Land of Promise,* 1939; Rupert N. Richardson, Adrian Anderson, and Ernest Wallace, Texas, *The Lone Star State,* Seventh Edition, 1997 (First Edition, 1943); T.R. Feherenbach, *Lone Star,* 1968 (often used as a college textbook); Robert A. Calvert and Arnoldo DeLeon, *The History of Texas,* 1996; Randolph B. Campbell, *Gone to Texas, A History of The Lone Star State,* 2003. *Regulator-Moderator War, An East Texas Feud, 1840-1844,* by Leila B. LaGrone of Carthage was privately printed in 1995.

[12]Fischer, Robert Potter, 6.

[13]Fischer, Robert Potter, 4.

[14]Arrington, *Rangers and Regulators of the Tanaha,* vii.

[15] Arrington, *Rangers and Regulators of the Tanaha,* 168, 179.

[16]Kirkland, *Love is a Wild Assault,* 12.

[17]Ashcroft ms, Preface page.

# Bibliography

## Primary Sources

Ames, Harriet A. "The History of Harriet A. Ames During the Early Days of Texas." Manuscript in the archives of the Jefferson Historical Museum.

Ashcroft, Dr. Levi Henderson. "The History of the War Between the Regulators and Moderators of Shelby County." Unpublished manuscript, ca. 1853. Fondren Library, Southern Methodist University, Dallas.

Daggett, Eph M. "Recollections of the War of the Moderators and Regulators."Unpublished manuscript, available at the Shelby County Historical Museum, Center.

1850 Census, Shelby County, Texas. Transcribed by Kathryn Davis for the Shelby County Historical Society, Center.

1860 Census, Shelby County, Texas. Transcribed by Kathryn Davis for the Shelby County Historical Society, Center.

Gulick, Charles Adams, Jr., *et al*, eds. *The Papers of Mirabeau Buonaparte Lamar*, Vol. III. Austin: The Pemberton Press, 1968.

*Harrison County District Court, Civil Minutes*, Vol. A.

*Harrison County District Court, Civil Minutes*, Vol. B.

Sam Malone, ed. *A. Horton – Patriot of the Republic of Texas.* San Augustine: S. Malone, Printer, 1984.

*Journals, Sixth Congress, Republic of Texas*, Vol. I.

Lack, Paul, ed. *The Diary of William Fairfax Gray, From Virginia to Texas, 1835 –1837.* Dallas: De Golyer Library & William P. Clements Center for Southwest Studies,Southern Methodist University, 1997.

Middleton, John W. *History of the Regulators and Moderators and the Shelby County War in 1841 and 1842, in the Republic of Texas.* Fort Worth: Loving Publishing Company, 1883.

Smith, Edward. "Account of a Journey Through Northern Texas." *East Texas Historical Journal*, Vol. VII, No. 2, October 1969

Thompson, _____. Killing of John M. Bradley. Handwritten recollection in the San Augustine Public Library.

White, Gifford. *1840 Census of Texas, Land Grants,* Vol. III. Austin: 1988.

Williams, Amelia W., and Eugene C. Barker, eds. *The Writings of Sam Houston,* 6 vols. Austin: University of Texas Press, 1938-1943.

## Books

Abernethy, Francis Edward, et al, eds. *The Family Saga, A Collection of Texas Family Legends.* Denton: University of North Texas Press, 2003.

Arrington, Alfred W. (pseud. of Charles Summerfield). *The rangers and regulators of the Tanaha; or, life among the lawless. A tale of the republic of Texas.* New York: Robert M. DeWitt, publisher, 1856. (Reprinted in New York in 1874 with Mayne Reid as listed author.)

Boorman, Dean K. *Guns of the Old West, An Illustrated History.* Guilford, Connecticut: The Lyons Press, 2002.

Bowman, Bob and Doris. *More Historic Murders of East Texas.* Lufkin: Best of East Texas Publishers, 2004.

Brown, John Henry. *History of Texas, From 1685 to 1892.* Austin: Jenkins Publishing Company Inc., 1892.

Brown, Richard Maxwell. *Strain of Violence, Historical Studies of American Violence and Vigilantism.* New York: Oxford University Press, 1975.

Cash, W. J. *The Mind of the South.* New York: Alfred A. Knopf, Inc., 1941.

Combs, Joseph F. *Gunsmoke in the Redlands.* San Antonio: The Naylor Company, 1968.

Crocket, G. L. *Two Centuries in East Texas.* Dallas: The Southwest Press, 1932

Dedera, Don. *A Little War of Our Own, The Pleasant Valley War Revisited.* Flagstaff, Arizona: Northland Press, 1

Douglas, C.L. *Famous Texas Feuds.* Dallas: Turner Company, 1936.

Esposito, Brigadier General Vincent J., ed. *The West Point Atlas of American Wars,* Vol. I, 1689-1981. New York: Henry Holt and Company, 1995.

Fischer, Ernest G. *Robert Potter, Founder of the Texas Navy.* Gretna, LA: Pelican Publishing Company, 1976.

Forrest, Earle R. *Arizona's Dark and Bloody Ground.* Caldwell,
Idaho: The Caxton Printers, Ltd., 1950.

Gard, Wayne. *Frontier Justice* Norman: University of Oklahoma
Press, 1949.

Hansen, Harry, ed. *Texas, A Guide to the Lone Star State.* New Revised
Edition. New York: Hastings House, Publishers, 1969.

Hogan, William Ransom. *The Texas Republic.* Austin: University
of Texas Press, 1969.

Hollon, W. Eugene. *Frontier Violence, Another Look.* New York:
Oxford University Press, 1974.

Johnson, David. *The Mason County "Hoo Doo" War, 1874-1902.*
Denton: University of North Texas Press, 2006.

Jones, Virgil Carrington. *The Hatfields and the McCoys.* Chapel
Hill: The University of North Carolina Press, 1948.

Kemp. L.W. *The Signers of the Texas Declaration of Independence.*
Houston: The Anson Jones Press, 1944.

Kirkland, Elithe Hamilton. *Love is a Wild Assault.* Garden City,
N.Y.: Doubleday & Company, Inc., 1959.

LaGrone, Leila B., *et al. A History of Panola County, Texas, 1819-
1978.* Carthage: Panola Historical Association, 1979.

LaGrone Leila B. *Regulator Moderator War, An East Texas Feud,
1840-1844.* Carthage: Panola County Historical and
Genealogical Association, 1995.

McLean, Rev. John H. *Reminiscences.* Dallas: Smith & Lamar, 1918.

Moore, Wyatt. *Every Sun That Rises.* Austin: University of Texas
Press, 1985.

Nevin, David. *The Mexican War.* Alexandria, Virginia: Time-Life
Books, 1978.

Nichols, Edward J. *Zach Taylor's Little Army.* Garden City, N.Y.:
Doubleday & Company, Inc., 1963.

Nix, Bennie E. *Shelby County – Part of Her Early History; Soldiers
Serving From Shelby County in 1846-1848, United States-
Mexican War, Biographical Sketches,* N.p., 1964.

Nix, Bennie E. *Shelby County – Part of Her Early Story; County
Officers, Members of Congress, Republic of Texas, Members of
Legislature, Reconstruction Era.* N.p., n.d.

Nolan, Frederick. Bad Blood, *The Life and Times of the Horrell
Brothers.* Stillwater, Oklahoma: Barbed Wire Pres, 1994.

Oglesbee, John and Betty. *San Augustine: A Texas Treasure.*
Nacogdoches: East Texas Historical Association, 2001.

O'Neal, Bill. *The Bloody Legacy of Pink Higgins, A Half Century of Violence in Texas.* Austin: Eakin Press, 1999.

O'Neal, Bill. *Cattlemen vs. Sheepherders, Five Decades of Violence In the West,* Austin: Eakin Press, 1989.

O'Neal, Bill. *The Johnson County War.* Austin: Eakin Press, 2004.

O'Neal, Bill. *Tex Ritter, America's Most Beloved Cowboy.* Austin: Eakin Press, 1998.

Panola County Historical Survey Committee. *Pioneer Panola County.* Carthage: Panola County Commissioners' Court, 1976.

Phares, Ross. *Reverend Devil, A Biography of John A. Murrell.* New Orleans: Pelican Publishing Company, 1941.

Pinkston, Mildred Cariker. *People, Places, Happenings, Shelby County, Texas.* Center: Pinkston Books, 1985.

Prassel, Frank Richard. *The Great American Outlaw, A Legacy of Fact and Fiction.* Norman: University of Oklahoma Press, 1993.

Rice, Otis K. *Hatfields and the McCoys.* Lexington: University Press of Kentucky, 1978.

Rinaldi, Ann. *The Coffin Quilt: The Feud between the Hatfields and the McCoys.* San Diego: Harcourt Brace, 1999.

Sanders, J.B. *Hangings in Shelby County,* Center: N.p., 1966.

Sanders, Leonard. *How Forth Worth Became the Texasmost City, 1849-1920.* Fort Worth: Texas Christian University Press, 1973.

Shearer, Ernest C. *Robert Potter, Remarkable North Carolinian and Texan.* Houston: University of Houston Press, 1951.

Sonnichsen, C.L. *I'll Die Before I'll Run, The Story of the Great Feuds of Texas.* New York: Devin-Adair, 1962.

Sonnichsen, C.L. *Ten Texas Feuds.* Albuquerque: University of New Mexico Press, 1957.

Tyler, Ron, Ed.-in-Chief. *The New Handbook of Texas.* 6 Vols. Austin: The Texas State Historical Association, 1996.

Weber, Charles W. *Jack Long; or, shot in the Eye. A true story of Texas border life.* New York: W.H. Graham, 1846.

Worman, Charles G. *Gunsmoke and Saddle Leather, Firearms in the Nineteenth Century American West.* Albuquerque: University of New Mexico Press, 2005.

Yoakum, Henderson. *History of Texas, From Its First Settlement in 1685 to Its Annexation to the United States in 1846.* New York: Redfield, 1855.

# Articles

Atterbury, Eleanor. "The Bloody Neutral Ground in Harrison County." *Texas History Teachers Magazine,* Vol. XIV.

Britton, Hazel Miller. "Stories My Grandmother Told Me." *East Texas Historical Journal,* Vol. VIII, 1970.

Clark, Edward. "The Regulator-Moderator War." *The Texas Gulf* `History Society,* Vol. I, No. 1.

Culbertson, Gilbert M. "The Regulators and Moderators: A Tale of Old Tenaha." *Texana,* Vol. XII, No. 1, 1974.

Hogan William. "Rampant Individualism in the Republic of Texas." *Southwestern Historical Quarterly,* Vol. XLV, No. 4, April 1941.

Horgan, Paul. "The Lost Journals of a Southwestern Frontiersman," *Southwestern Historical Quarterly,* Vol. XLIV, No. 1, July 1940.

Marshall, Mrs. Arch B. "History Of The Brittain Family Who Came To Shelby County In 1837." *The Champion,* Center, January 24, 196

McLean, John H. "A Famous Murder of 1842, Rose-Potter." *Texas Methodist Historical Quarterly,* Vol. II, No. 1, July 1910.

Murray, Joe. "Memories Live in the Mind of East Texas." *Panola Watchman,* Carthage, August 15, 1969.

Nixon, Pat Ireland. "Judge Alfred W. Arrington, Judge William H. Rhodes, and the Case of Summerfield." *Southwestern Historical Quarterly,* Vol. LV, No. 3, January 1952.

Roberts, O.M. "The Shelby County War, or the Regulators and Moderators." *Texas Magazine,* August 1897.

Ruffin, Thomas. "The Elusive East Texas Border." *East Texas Historical Journal,* Vol. XI, 1973.

Sanders, Leon, ed. "A Letter from East Hamilton." *East Texas Historical Journal,* Vol. XXVIII, No. 2, Fall 1990.

Tatum, James. "The Muses of Jefferson." *Southwest Review,* Vol. 69, No. 3, Summer 1984.

## Newspapers

Clarksville *Northern Standard*
Galveston *News*
Houston *Democratic Telegraph and Texas Register*
Houston *Morning Star*
Marshall *News-Messenger*
Niles' *Weekly Register*
San Augustine *Redlander*

## Miscellaneous

Armstrong, James Curtis. "The History of Harrison County, Texas, 1839 to 1880." M.A. Thesis, Stephen F. Austin State Teachers College, Nacogdoches, 1926.

Biographical Files, Harrison County Historical Society, Marshall.

Clark, Edward. "The Regulator-Moderator War." An Address Delivered at the February 18, 1965, Meeting of the Daughters of the Republic of Texas in Beaumont.

Davidson, Judge T. Whitfield. "The Fate of Robert Potter, The Trial of Charles W, Jackson, The War of the Regulators and Moderators." N.p., n.d.

District Officers. Vertical File, Harrison County Historical Society, Marshall.

Garrett, Gilbert. Interview by the author, Garrett cabin near San Augustine. November 17, 2005

Hargrove, Johnny. Multiple interviews by the author, Shelbyville, January and February, 2006.

Key, Cdr. Hobart, Jr. The International Boundary Park, Pamphlet. Marshall, Texas: Port Caddo Press, 1976.

Love, John Warren. "The Regulator-Moderator Movement in Shelby County, Texas." M.A. Thesis, The University of Texas, 1936.

McCrocklin, Claude. Archaeology Report on Tests at the Robert Potter-Harriet Ames Site 41MR51 on Potter's Point, Caddo Lake, Texas. June 2000.

Neill, Lela Rhodes. "Episodes in the Early History of Shelby County." M.A. Thesis, Stephen F. Austin State College, 1950.

Person, Annette Sanders, Letter to Bob Bowman, November 8, 2004.

Pertula, Timothy K. Archaeological Investigations at the Robert

Potter and Harriet Ames Cabin, Site 41MR51 on Potter's Point, Caddo Lake. N.d.

Porter, Mary Jane Brittain. Application File for Official Texas Historical Marker for   Elder William Brittain and Wife, Rosanna Wright Brittain. Presented to Texas Historical Commission, 1980.

Sharp, Laurence R. "History of Panola County, Texas, to 1860." M.A. Thesis, The University of Texas, 1940.

Shelby County, General Land Office Map, Austin, Texas.

Youngblood, Dowell. Interview by the author, Shelby County Historical Museum, Center. November 16, 2005.

# INDEX